GENE'S Genes

*Betsy
Cheers
Gene*

AN AUTOBIOGRAPHY
By Francis Eugene O'Neil, Jr.

ISBN: 978-1-944293-32-1

Published in 2019. Albuquerque, New Mexico, USA

"The pessimist sees the difficulty in every opportunity, an optimist sees the opportunity in every difficulty".

- Winston Churchill

Acknowledgements

I am a very lucky man and virtually always an optimist... not sure which came first, luck or optimism!

I have a wonderful genetic inheritance from my parents Florence and Gene, their parents and their parents plus nearly a dozen aunts and uncles from my family and Sandy's family leading me to a life of fulfillment.

Sandy, our sons Mike, Steve, Dave, our daughter Sara, their spouses and their children are the family I had always hoped for and I am very proud of them.

The marriage and family of Gene and Sandy may never have developed except for the love of two other special people. Sandy's aunt Mary Ellen Miller and my uncle, Don Bolier, who in the 1950's each gave our romance a gentle nudge in their own special way.

Like brothers I never had, Bill Bonesho, Jim Scolman, Ted Bergstrom, Harland Sievert, cousin Neil Norelius, Jack Allison (D), George Losby, BTTE (D) Bob Neperud (D), Jim Nichols, Tom Hanson (D), and Rex Bolick (D) have all been close friends, some since 1940 and have helped shape my life.

There are many more who guided and mentored me and some who were good enough at their life for me to just observe and attempt to emulate them.

The 1943-1953 staff at the Eau Claire YMCA including Clayton Anderson and Vic Johnson; Sgt. Bill Haugen, US Air Force 1954; Dr John Thurston and Dr. Dick Hibbard, U

Wisconsin, Eau Claire 1960; Jim Murphy and Dick Converse at Honeywell, Aero 1964; Lee Harness at Graco, 1968; Lloyd Towner, Tom Zosel, Jerry Paar and Roger Stangland at Coast to Coast Hardware 1975; Ted Bergstrom an entrepreneur and business partner 1977; Steve Fredrickson my go-to guy at the failing Energy Shed, 1983; Attorney Vern Vanderweid at Wiese and Cox Law firm 1980; and Yale Dolginow, Paper Warehouse, 1994 all made huge contributions to my life. Many thanks to all for the education and sharing of your know-how.

I also want to thank the people who helped make this book happen. It all started with cousins Marilyn Stutt, Georgia Clausen, Gail Skinner and Patti Main. Sandy and I drove down to Albuquerque for Marilyn's big 90th birthday celebration. The night before the party, we had dinner with the "girls," and I was telling them about our trips to Ireland and how we'd been finding out so much about our ancestors. They were fascinated, and insisted I think about putting it all down in a book.

I laughed it off that evening, but then at Marilyn's birthday party the next night, Sandy and I found ourselves answering dozens of questions about family history, the roots of the early families in the UK and in their early Wisconsin pioneer days. We have made several Ireland trips and visited the exact site of the O'Neil's home property in County Kerry. The extended family seemed to have an insatiable thirst for more information and provoked me by suggesting that our grandchildren and their grandchildren would benefit from a written record of what we have learned.

In the following weeks, Cousin Marilyn Stutt was especially encouraging of my putting it all down in a book. She had spent 20 years in the publishing business, and thought it was a worth-while project. She is also a motivator. I couldn't refuse. I sat down to my computer and started typing. To my surprise, the stories just seemed to write themselves, and before the year was up, I had a manuscript for Marilyn to edit. Next, she did her design magic and I had a book ready for the printer. She not only got my heartfelt thanks, but I threw in a few hugs, besides.

I also need to thank cousin Patti Bolier Helgeson, daughter of Uncle Don Bolier, who supplied photos and family information on the Boliers for my story.

Oldest Son Mike has been of specific help in preparing the many photographs published in the photo section of the book. These photos help tell the story beginning with the loggers, in the primary industry of northern Wisconsin in the late 1800's up to and including late 2018.

And lastly, to my early family, all of whom made contributions to my genetic makeup I say thanks for the dominant genes, some Irish, some French, some English and some Scottish. These have led to a long life with no bad diseases, a high capacity for love and friendship, patience, courage to venture and try new ways, a high level of energy to stay focused on worthy projects and to drop projects which have become unworthy.

I owe thanks to so many.

Introduction

At an early age in the 1940's I became aware of family history mostly by overhearing my parents, aunts, uncles and grandparents speak of their youth. Equally fascinating were their references to their parents (my Great Grandparents) links to the old country, Ireland, England, Scotland and France and their immigration to attain the "better life" for the family as pioneers in the USA.

Had those pioneers known how long it would take for the "better life" to occur, some may have been quite discouraged.

Though the USA and Canada offered free homestead land and many other benefits, it was not easy to attain the "better life" many immigrants sought. The US Civil War in the 1860's cost the lives of tens of thousands of volunteer and conscripted Irishmen. Economic problems of the 1880's, World War I in 1914-1918, the Great Depression of 1929-1941, World War II, and the Korean War not ending until 1953 all contributed to nearly a century of hardship.

In later years I scolded myself for missing such an opportunity to ask the many important questions about the family in the "old days." Since becoming an adult, my curiosity led to travels to the New England states in search of information about these families. Arthur and Julia O'Neil from County Kerry in Ireland, the James and Margaret Orr's from Scotland and Manchester, England and the Fred and Delia Bolier families from French Canada. Each family has a New England connection in the mid 1800's.

As adults, Sandy and I have traveled to Ireland on three occasions and at last stood on the very ground of the O'Neil farm in Cromane, a tiny community in County Kerry near Tralee, the Dingle Peninsula and the Ring of Kerry.

I picked up two small stones and a bit of gravel from the site of the O'Neil place and, on my return to the site of their graves in Wolf Creek, Polk County, Wisconsin, placed the treasures on their 100-year-old gravestone. Silly me, it was like a religious ceremony.

Connecting these "Roots" to the lives Gene and Sandra O'Neil have carved out for our family in the 1940's-2018, is the subject of this book, I call it my autobiography. I have no siblings but many cousins who have asked "Do you have it written down for the benefit of the extended families in later years"? The answer was no, but I will do it in 2018!

I share it with anyone interested in our family history, a slice of Western Wisconsin history, a love story of Sandra Lou Tietge and Francis Eugene O'Neil and their marriage of over 60 years. Sons Mike, Steve and Dave, daughter Sara, their spouses Susanne Busse, Christine Anderson, Betty Scott, Rich Fish and grandchildren Becky, Katy, Madeline, Megan, Nick O'Neil and Sandra Fish, all-in-the-family.

For a guy who nearly flunked English Composition 101 in the first semester of college, this has been a writing challenge to me. But I am ok with the completed work and hopeful that some time a family member will pick up the book and find an "Ah-Ha" in its pages.

But, thank you my family for the inherited gifts of good-health, ambition, personal energy, courage, emotion, fair play, resourcefulness, love, compassion and a passion for ventures. I hope my "good genes" will pass on to those who follow.

Table of Contents

Chapter 1   "ROOTS" AND PIONEERS   1

Chapter 2   ECONOMIC HARD TIMES AND WORLD WAR II   23

Chapter 3   LIFE POST WAR   45

Chapter 4   THE AIR FORCE, MARRIAGE AND BEYOND   59

Chapter 5   CORPORATE AMERICA: A GREAT UNIVERSITY   83

Chapter 6   THE RISE AND FALL OF THE ENERGY SHED VENTURE   107

Chapter 7   OTHER OPPORTUNITIES COME KNOCKING   131

Chapter 8   ANNUAL DEER HUNTING - A FAMILY TRADITION   143

Chapter 9   RETIREMENT – DOING IT "OUR WAY"   155

Chapter 1
"ROOTS" AND PIONEERS

THE O'NEILS

My family history goes back to the early 1800's and is predominately Irish, Scotch, English and French. Though O'Neil is a common name in Ireland, my branch of O'Neils have their history in Southwest Ireland in County Kerry, the villages of Cromane, Killorglin and Blennerville, all of which are near Tralee and not far from Killarney. This area of Ireland, with a history of 8,000 years, is especially scenic and historic. It's located between the Dingle Peninsula, and The Ring of Kerry on the Atlantic Ocean at Castlemaine Harbour.

The town of Dingle is a charming fishing village. The peninsula is sprinkled with ageless limestone igloos, formerly the Monks living quarters, used and abandoned hundreds of years ago. The Ring of Kerry is a scenic drive through the hills and on virtually every visitor's list of "Do not miss" sites in Western Ireland. The Ring is home of the McGillycuddy Reeks, another don't miss for tourists.

Though O'Neil is a common name in Ireland, ours is spelled with just one L, unlike most Irish spelling with two L's. It may be a Catholic/Church-of-Ireland thing but our family uses just one L, and family members were always quick to add "and it makes one "L" of a difference."

A group of O'Neills spelling their name with two "L's" were a dominant family in Northern Ireland during the 1600's. They were referred to as the "Kings" and mostly resided in County Tyrone. These O'Neills have their fingerprints all over Donegal Castle in Northern Ireland and in historical story-boards in the museum located inside the city walls of Londonderry (Derry), Northern Ireland. Near Derry, a fortress of rock and stone exists on a hill, which the O'Neills of the time erected for protection of their clan.

The O'Neil Crest has face-to-face Lions tussling over a red hand above a body of water. It's known as the "Red Hand of Ulster." According to Irish lore, the kingdom of Ulster had at one time no rightful heir. Because of this, it was agreed that a boat race should take place and that "whosoever's hand is the first to touch the shore of Ireland, so shall he be made the king".

The potential king from the O'Neill clan so desired the kingship that, upon seeing that he was losing the race, cut off his hand and threw it to the shore — thus winning the kingship. It has become a symbol of Ireland, Ulster, and other places associated with the ruling family of O'Neills.

The Red Hand of Ulster has become an important symbol in Northern Ireland, (sometimes of defiance) and is seen frequently in our travels. It has attracted such popular symbolism that it may be found in many places other than Northern Ireland, including a certain St. Paul, Minnesota, Irish Pub on University Ave.

***

My great-grandfather, Arthur Alfred O'Neil, was born in 1819, the son of Edward Neill and Lucy Blennerhassett, both of Cromane. The O'Neils were farmers and shopkeepers, The Blennerhassett's were statesmen, soldiers and one a member of parliament. The Blennerhasset family lived in a castle and founded the town and seaport of Blennerville. The castle, with a history back to 1590, operates even today, near Tralee as the elegant Ballyseedy Castle Hotel.

In 1846, Arthur married Julia Langford, born in 1827, ... twice ... in one month ... in the Catholic Church and the Church of Ireland Church. (Apparently the families did not approve of mixed marriages.) The family of my Great Grandmother Julia were listed as farmers.

By 1849, during the potato famine, Arthur and Julia and infant sons, Edward and William, were living in Cromane, a small village near Castlemaine Harbor in Co. Kerry. Times were terrible according to the history records. English land owners were swarming Ireland, taking over land, evicting small farmers unable to meet the stiff requirements of their mortgages or rents and burning their homes. Simultaneously, the English were harvesting and shipping Irish produce and farm products back to England leaving the Irish to survive on the lowly potato. The English were raping the Irish forests of high-quality timber and shipping it to England for the production of lumber to build English buildings. Westminster Abby is built of Irish Oak! Even today the reforestation of Ireland is incomplete, though underway and managed.

The potato contracted the blight. Potatoes rotted in the fields, seed potatoes were devoured by the starving people to stay alive until the next year's crop could be harvested. There was no next year's crop, and the little country faced mass starvation. In England, the civil authorities refused Irish cries for help because they did not want the lowly Irish "dependent on them!" Queen Victoria may have been sympathetic but not sufficiently enthusiastic to order the substantial emergency aid needed. Irish children were dying, their parents, helpless, right behind them.

The potato famine killed one million Irish and forced two million to leave their homeland for North America and South America, Canada and Australia. So many deaths occurred enroute, the ships became known as "Coffin Ships." . . . And the English slept . . . and ignored their cries.

Arthur, Julia, and their two infant sons left their homeland in the late 1840's for a two-thousand-mile trip to North America. This was an incredible amount of courage leaving home, family, friends and possessions. And, never likely to return. We believe they departed from the port at Blennerville, a port, which was right near their home in Cromane. They reached North America at an undetermined port and lived in Keene and Westmorland New Hampshire and in London Ontario, Canada for the next 30 years. More children were born including number thirteen, Charles Francis, my Grandfather, born in London Ontario, Canada in 1871.

Canada was seeing a large number of immigrants from Europe. Like the USA, the vastness of the USA and Canada was hard for newly arriving immigrants to comprehend. Canada, and the USA began to offer settlers incentives for settling in the heartland, which included free passage and free land.

The O'Neil family, possibly motivated by the Canadian incentives but also by the American Civil War, elected to relocate to London, Ontario Canada. After some years in Canada, the family relocated to the United States, residing in Minneapolis for a short time. In 1882, they homesteaded on a wooded acreage in the valley of the St Croix River in Burnett County, Wisconsin. The home was located midway between St Croix Falls and Grantsburg, Wisconsin, just two miles east of the scenic St. Croix, River.

Little did they know the soil conditions of the area supported timber growth but was very poor for agricultural crops. They were in the valley of the St Croix River, which at the time of the last glacier was deposited with tremendous depths of fine sugar sand throughout the valley. That fine sand does not make good ground for grains and vegetables.

The homestead was abandoned by the family in the 1920's after the deaths of Arthur and Julia, and the energy of son John O'Neil was spent. Arthur and Julia are buried in the Wolf Creek Cemetery just 8 miles to the south of the homestead site. The only marks still visible of the original home are a depression in the ground marking the outline and depth of the cellar of the home.

THE ORRS AND THE ROGERS

James Orr, Sr., was born in 1798 near Manchester, England. He married Margaret Carmichael of Dundee, Scotland and in 1820, they immigrated to Aroostook County, Maine. Margaret soon died, and in 1822, he married her sister, Jane Carmichael, who had been born in 1799 in Dundee, Scotland.

James Orr Jr. was born June 24,1829 in Aroostook, Co. Maine, near Haynesville. He married Margaret Rogers June 24,1851 at the Baptist Church in Aroostook Co. Maine. They had eight children while farming in rock-infested rural Maine.

Robert and Tom Rogers, Margaret's brothers, went West and homesteaded in the St Croix Falls, Wisconsin, area about 1861. James Orr, their brother-in-law, followed about 1864 leaving his family behind while he arranged for homestead land and proceeded to build a home for his family of eight children.

In July 1866, Margaret Rogers Orr traveled to Wisconsin from Calais, Maine with her eight children. The journey included travel by boat from Calais, Maine, to Portland, then by train to the largest waterway nearby, followed by water through the Great Lakes to the "Small City of Chicago" (as described in the family records). Then, by train to Galena, Illinois, and boarded another river boat heading north on the Mississippi, to the St Croix River, to the final landing at Franconia, Minnesota, located between Stillwater, Minnesota, and St Croix Falls, Wisconsin.

It was here that Margaret "arrived with eight sick children" and was met at the pier in Franconia (or Marine on the St Croix) to a happy reunion of the family. The family loaded up on the horse drawn wagon for the last leg of the trip to their log home in Sterling Township, Polk Co Wisconsin, a distance of about 30 miles. Sterling Township was located in the river valley of the St Croix River and two miles east of the river, fifteen miles north of St. Croix Falls.

It was 1864, and just 20-30 years after the first "Whites" began to settle in the area. Life was not easy for the settlers. The earth was flat and free of stones, but as a spillway for the melted glacial water from the glacier of 10,000 years ago, soil conditions were so bad they were unable to support crop growth. Timber and logging were the primary industry of the area. The Great White Pine forest covered hundreds of thousands of acres in Wisconsin, Minnesota and Michigan with an upper canopy of dense pine growth, which prevented the sun from ever reaching the forest floor. There was no undergrowth.

MAGGIE & CHARLIE O'NEIL

September 15, 1872 in their "old log house on the meadow" in the town of Sterling, Polk Co Wisconsin – Margaret (Maggie), was born the twelfth child in the family which ultimately grew to 13 children. Maggie was my grandmother, a true pioneer child living on the edge of the wilderness.

In 1882, the family moved to a new log house just a few miles northwest of the village of Cushing, Wisconsin. The house was larger but still at the edge of white civilization. It was notable, however, that the house was above the riverbed of the St Croix and in soil much more suitable for crop farming than the original location.

Maggie and her mother, Margaret, were cooks in the lumber camps while her dad and brothers were lumberjacking in the nearby forests. She was teaching country school at the age of 17 in the area of Sunrise, Minnesota and later in the area of Cushing Wisconsin. To this day there is an "Orr School" building located near Cushing, Wisconsin.

Maggie endured many hardships. The families of the area, whose children would attend the school, would see to it a large pile of firewood was available to the teacher just outside the door. The teacher, who was often living in one of the nearby homes of a student, would trudge her way to the school in the early morning, haul in the firewood, build the fire to warm up the one room school and prepare for a day of teaching all from first graders to eighth graders.

The schools were built with a cloak-room separated from the teaching room by a partial wall. This room must be heated as well, because the children's lunches were stashed in this room. The pint of milk brought from home in a mason jar for lunch must be kept from freezing, and the boots and snow clothes worn to school must get dry before the end of the school day.

And for this ... Maggie was paid $22-$27.00 per month.

Maggie was bright, pretty and outgoing, Charlie O'Neil was handsome and ambitious. In the 1890's two young people born just one year apart; each children of pioneer families with origins in the United Kingdom; each living within a few miles of each other at the edge of a vast wilderness; each affiliated with the Protestant Church of England/Ireland ... found each other.

Maggie was musical and played the violin, organ and piano. She was a skilled writer for her time, authoring a book about the history of the St. Croix Valley in pioneer days and wrote for the community newspaper for many years. Charlie played the violin and had a good singing voice. It should come as no surprise that they courted and married May 4,1897. They celebrated their 50th anniversary in 1947, and all seven grandchildren attended.

On September 1, 1901, Charles Francis O'Neil and Margaret L. O'Neil entered into an agreement with Skeffington Burns of the village of St Croix Falls. They pledged the following personal property to secure a $100 note (I have the deed in my collection). The intended use of the money is unknown but it was possibly applied to a venture of Charlies since about this time he was launching a meat market in St Croix Falls.

As collateral: ONE RED COW, AGE TWO (2) YEARS, TWO RED COWS (3) YEARS OLD, ONE BLACK MULEY COW (3) YEARS OLD (and six more cows listed similarly.) ALL SAID COWS BEING NOW IN THE PASTURE ON THE SW 1/4 OF SECTION

3, TOWNSHIP 34, RANGE 20 IN THE TOWN OF GRANTSBURG, BURNETT COUNTY, WISCONSIN.

Maggie and Charlie lived in a home on the main street of St. Croix Falls. Charlie died in 1954. Maggie spent several more years there before going into the nursing home in Amery, Wisconsin. On her final trip to St Croix Falls in May of 1963, just days before she passed away, she requested the driver of the ambulance drive her past her old house. She had enough strength to get up on her elbows to have one last look. Charlie and Maggie are both buried in the St Croix Falls Cemetery.

Maggie and Charlie had three children: Francis Eugene, (My Dad) born October 6, 1905, in St Croix Falls, Wisconsin, died in Eau Claire, Wisconsin, November 14,1975, at 70 years of age. He is buried in the Baldwin Wisconsin cemetery. He and My Mother were married on July 14, 1933 and had just one child, me! At his death My mother Florence, her sister Hazel, his Sister Carol and I were present when he took his last breath.

Margaret (Peg) Julia was born June 5, 1908 in St Croix Falls, Wisconsin. Died January 30, 2000 at 92 years in Albuquerque, NM. She married Myron (Mike) Heebink of Baldwin, Wisconsin. They had four daughters, Marilyn, Nancy, Georgia and Gail.

(Note: Sandy and I were fortunate to visit Aunt Peg in Albuquerque just days before she died. She was quite spry that day and was looking forward to our visit. Shortly after we left town, she passed away. It was as if she willed herself to stay alive until after our visit.)

Carol Rebecca was born December 25, 1910, in St Croix Falls, Wisconsin. Died at 96 on April 12, 2006, in Lindstrom, Minnesota. She Married Paul Norelius, from a line of early Swedish settlers in the area of Lindstrom. They had two sons, Neil and Jay. She was loving to a fault and exceptionally gifted in music where she played tunes endlessly from the 20's, 30's and 40's all from memory and without printed music!

(Note: Carol loved babies. In late March of 2006, Sandy, Madeline (Son Mike and Susanne's daughter) Sara and I went to the nursing home to visit Aunt Carol and show her our new granddaughter, Sandra Jean Fish, barely one month old. Carol took this little baby in her arms and smooched her and spoke to, her and hugged her and passed on some "real love". She was an expert at machine-gun kisses. She read Madeline's palm that day and told her good things were coming to her.)

MARGARET (MAGGIE) ORR O'NEIL

Born number 12 of 13 Children in Polk Co. Wisconsin on September 15 1872 in a large family where personal drive, motivation, ambition and a strong will could lead you to a promising life. She had it all, high achiever, well known, popular and contributor to the community. Maggie was an outstanding baker. She did all her baking in an old wood/coal burning kitchen range and turned out the finest bread, rolls, cookies and cakes. She turned out extraordinary doughnuts. She was a top seamstress, a newspaper reporter and a mystic.

She was a seamstress of great skill making patchwork quilts of bits of men's wool suits. When my father was five years old in 1910 and considered a mascot for the St. Croix Falls town baseball team, she made him a full baseball uniform. Little britches reaching just below the knees, a shirt with the SCF team logo, a warm-up jacket with two pockets, the team logo on the sleeve and MASCOT in coordinating color letters sewn on the front of the jacket. Even a tiny baseball cap with sun-visor. We have the whole outfit in our collection.

Maggie was a regular weekly contributor to the "The Standard Press", the local St. Croix Falls newspaper, where her insight and humor would leak out of her articles. She read palms, tea-leaves and cards. Often towns-people would come by for a session and frequently bring their friends and visitors. If a customer was having a personal problem, Maggie would always find some good news in the leaves for that person before they left the house. After they were gone, she would say. "Well, they have been here before, they must like what they hear."

She and Charlie were musical. Maggie played the old pump organ and Charlie the 1839 violin, which may have come over from Ireland with his family in the 1840's. (Note, Charlie on the violin was a bit of a stretch. He was a carpenter and stone-mason with hard and rough hands. Yet, he had a delicate touch on the violin.)

Most of all, Grandma Maggie was a loving grandma with hugs and machine-gun smooches. After a usual episode of smooches, she would say, "Too many kisses will make you sick," followed by a giggle.

CHARLES (CHARLIE) FRANCIS O'NEIL

Charlie was born in London Ontario Canada in 1871 he died in 1954, and is buried along-side Maggie in the St Croix Falls Cemetery. Charlie was the youngest of 13 children in the family.

In my collection of family memorabilia, I have the text-book, "Bricklaying," by Owen B. McGinnis and in his own familiar handwriting, "Chas O'Neil" "1890" is scrawled on the inside first page of the book. In 1890, Charlie was 19 years old and beginning the study of bricklaying and construction. It served him well because in 1954 at age 83, when he was suffering from the Cancer that would kill him, he announced to my dad that he could not afford to be sick, because he had "too damn much construction work lined up". He had laid his last brick, but he was not done, and his spirit was "damn the torpedoes... full speed ahead."

Among other projects, still visible in 2018, Charlie is credited with laying up the brick-work on the rural Deer Lake School located just East of St Croix Falls on Highway 8. He also was involved in the construction of a retaining wall on the North side of Highway 8, just West of the bridge at Taylors Falls. He worked on the construction of the hydro-electric dam of the St. Croix River, one-mile North of the bridge.

Charlie died of cancer in July 1954. Fortunately, I was home on leave from the Air Force and was able to attend the funeral. Charlie had a surprisingly varied and entrepreneurial career in construction shop-keeping, farm equipment sales and police work He was the top sales award winner in the early 1900's for being top salesman in the region of Northern Wisconsin by the International Harvester Farm Equipment Company. In the early 1900's, he developed and received a U. S. Patent for a device used in filling bags like those used for flour, farm feed, seed and fertilizer. He operated a meat market and kill yard in St Croix Falls, he bought and sold cattle and in the 1930's, 40's and 50's, he was elected and reelected several times to the position of Town Constable.

Charlie was also a dog trainer and received considerable Midwest area attention resulting from a two-page spread in the St Paul Pioneer Press newspaper about his wonder dog Paddy. Charlie and Paddy may have been the first K-9 police team in the country. Paddy was so famous, the town put the dog on the ballot one year and the dog nearly won.

Charlie had taught Paddy lots of tricks and some important jobs. He taught the dog to fetch particular tools from his toolbox. A saw, a hammer, a square, a mallet and other tools would be selected, and Paddy would deliver the right tool to Charley even up a ladder onto a roof.

Charlie was a kind and gentle cop. When he locked up a villain in the jailhouse, he would bring the villain lunch from the O'Neil family table.

WILLIAM (BILLY) ORR

One of Maggie's older brothers, William (Billy) Orr, born May 19, 1858 in Maine, was the most entrepreneurial member of their family. In the late 1800's the massive native White Pine forests of Northwestern Wisconsin, which seemed to be endless, were shrinking fast. As most of the Orrs and O'Neils worked in the woods prior to 1900 and massive amounts of big native timber was cut down and shipped to markets far and wide, the workers found it necessary to locate other work.

In about 1902-03, Billy Orr set out from the St Croix Falls area to find new territory for logging. Somehow, he found his way to a big, beautiful and bountiful Virgin White Pine forest near a lake north of the Iron Range in Northern Minnesota. He discovered the entire area was under the control of a particular Indian tribe.

He made a deal with the Tribal Chief to marry his daughter in exchange for rights to harvest the timber in the area.

He set up his lumber camps, arranged for a steamboat to be brought to the lake, (now Pelican Lake) and for railroad tracks to be brought up from Hibbing, Minnesota. His crews logged during the winter, and when the ice went out in Pelican Lake in the spring, made huge rafts of logs on the water and tugged them across the lake with his steamboat to the railroad siding. The logs were loaded onto the waiting railroad cars and shipped to the sawmill to be cut into fine virgin White Pine building materials much sought after by builders and contractors throughout the central United States.

Billy got rich! By 1905 he had founded the town and named it ORR, Minnesota. He owned the general store (still there) the saloon, hardware store, hotel, brothel and Chartered the bank in 1906. He would not permit a local church to start because he felt that might interfere with his saloon and brothel businesses.

With serendipity on my side Sandy and I discovered The General Store in Orr, owned several years in the 1970's by Eleanor and Phil Anshus. They worked hard to resurrect the magic of Billy and placed large pictures of Billy and his family in the store. Though they have since sold the store, even today a big picture in the store features Billy, his Native American wife and their daughter.

My sources about Billy include some from the family archives, but the family was not into bragging about Billy so I sought other sources. In 1962 when we moved to Minnesota, I met Ted Bergstrom who, through some 3M colleagues, had access to a deer hunting camp on Pelican Lake, at Orr. The camp and one mile of shoreline was owned by Monroe, an old fellow about 80 years old.

Ted invited me to join him hunting on this property near Orr, I believe we paid Monroe $3-4 per day to hunt on his land and sleep in his lakeside cabin. Our arrival at the camp always included a long visit with Monroe

Monroe had been in the Orr area many of his 80 plus years, including some years when Billy Orr was in business. He knew Billy and told the stories. He also told me Billy lost it all! He was a big drinker and, in Monroe's words, " He drank himself to death".

Eleanor Anshus suggested once I should go out North of Orr 2-3 miles to visit with another old-timer who had worked for Billy in the business. This was about in the 70's or 80's. This old timer was the son of the camp cook in Billy's camps. He said he was 12 years old when he went out to camp to work with his dad and Billy in the business. One remark stuck with me to this day. "The White Pine made such a dense canopy over the woods, there was no undergrowth". "You could walk for miles on pine needles."

St Croix Falls, Wisconsin
MELTING POT FOR THE O'NEILS, ORRS AND ROGERS

St Croix Falls, Wisconsin is a picturesque village located on a point where the river's flow was constricted by the landscape and huge Basalt outcroppings are visible. Ultimately a bridge was erected here and a hydroelectric generating dam just one mile upstream. The river was once mighty and dominated the landscape for many miles to the North as far as Lake Superior and the Duluth Harbor.

Even today, evidence of the fury of the pre-historic river may be observed. In Taylors Falls, Minnesota, just across the river from St. Croix Falls large potholes in the hard Basalt are visible reminders of the fury of the river. These potholes, the largest of which may be six to seven feet in diameter and sixty or more feet deep were ground out of the bluffs by a bloated river grinding deep pits in solid rock over a thousand years or longer.

The river was a principal outlet for huge amounts of ice melting from the last glacier about 10,000 years ago. Evidence of the southern edge of the last Glacier is noted in this area of Wisconsin by the nearby "Ice Age Trail", a popular hiking trail through Northern Wisconsin then heading south-east towards Southeastern Wisconsin.

The St Croix river was a main conduit for loggers to send their logs south to the sawmills in Stillwater. Each logging company would brand their trees then submit them to the river for a long float to Stillwater. Many huge log jams occurred where St Croix Falls and Taylors Falls, Minnesota meet.

The river valley 20 miles North of St Croix Falls shows the scars of a torrential flow of water over hundreds or thousands of years. The valley is four miles wide and hundreds of feet deep caused by the melting of the glacier 10,000 years earlier. The valley had great consequence for the pioneer settlers including the O'Neil and the Orr families. The ground beneath them was unsuitable for farming grains.

The O'Neil homestead and many more pioneer homesteads were located in the valley of sand. My Dad spoke of going up to the farm to help out his Uncle John during the summer and fall in about 1919. He said that about the only crop to grow in the sand soil was ryegrass. It was so hot and dry that the body was always uncomfortable except when uncle hooked up the horses to the wagon and went to town for supplies. The nearest town at the time was in Minnesota at Rush City. There was a ferry the settlers used that crossed the St Croix River to Rush City. As they approached the river, Dad would get out of the wagon, run up-river a few hundred yards and swim across. He recalled by swimming and using the river currents, he would arrive on the Rush City side about the same time uncle arrived on the shore crossing on the ferry.

THE BOLIER FAMILY

My Mother Florence's family, the Beaulieu (French spelling) family originally from France, had immigrated to Quebec, Canada in the early 1800's. In 1846, her grandfather, Pierre Beaulieu, (born in 1830-1905) and his new wife Delina Willett (1840-1923), relocated to Old Town, Maine, where they became inn-keepers. My grandfather, my mother's dad, Fred Bolier, (1879-1960) (Americanized spelling), and his two sisters, were born in Old Town, Maine, in 1879-1884. The family relocated from Maine to Minneapolis and then to near Spring Valley, Wisconsin, about 1885. Pierre was killed in an industrial accident there and is buried in a small cemetery near Spring Valley.

My grandfather, Fred, became the man of the house at a young age to support his mom, Delina, and two sisters. In the family records it's written that Fred worked very hard and saved $400, enough to purchase a home for his mom and sisters.

Delia Duhamel (1881-1930) my maternal grand-mother, also from a family of French-Canadian roots, was born in Dundas, Minnesota. She suffered from a heart condition for many years, dying in 1930. She is buried in the Hammond, Wisconsin,

Catholic Cemetery alongside Grandpa Fred. Her family had relocated from Canada to Dundas in the 1860's. Her father was a teacher.

Following her completion of school about 1887, Delia obtained housekeeping employment near Spring Valley, Wisconsin, and somehow met Fred, (perhaps through the Catholic Church). She and her family, including her dad Finley, mom Zoe and two brothers, relocated back to Canada. Later however, Delia returned to marry Fred Bolier in 1903 or 04. They had seven children.

FRED BOLIER, ENTREPREUNEUR

Fred owned a grocery and variety store on Main Street in Baldwin, Wisconsin. In 1907, Uncle Lloyd Bolier was born, soon followed by my mother, Florence, in 1908, Hazel in 1909 and Evelyn in 1912.

In 1911, Fred and Delia decided to relocate to Montana to homestead on land through the U.S. Government Homesteading program. Townsfolk in Baldwin called Fred a "Gentleman Farmer" and did not give him much credit for abilities to make it in the wide-open frontier of Montana. He was known as a merchant and real estate investor, not a farmer.

Well, Fred did a little farming but mostly he exercised his considerable business savvy in founding a store, a hotel/boarding house, a livery, a stage line and a meat market in Ballentine, Montana. This village remains a small community even today, but is well-located east of Billings and west of Custer and the Little Big Horn. Its claim to fame grew immensely in the early 1900's when the U.S. government developed an irrigation project bringing mountain water to the dry/arid Ballentine area. The family resided in the hotel for many years and another daughter, Marge, was born there in 1915.

The farm property, which was the original goal of the family relocation, was actually several miles out in the country near Stanford, located southeast of Great Falls, west of Lewistown, near the Lewis and Clark National Forest. The farmhouse was described as just "a big one room shack" and was never developed into a home by the Bolier family.

In 1916, the family was forced to return to Baldwin because Delia had a heart condition, which was severely aggravated by the altitude in Montana. It was a memorable Christmas for the family because they were all back together again in Baldwin," (Florence's words) With the family back in the hometown, my mother took on many of the parenting and domestic duties around the house during the remaining years of her mother's failing health.

Fred sold all the businesses he founded in Montana and accepted Montana land in exchange. There was a family rumor that he retained mineral rights to the underground minerals when the land sold including the oil rights. The truth to that has never been tested.

In 1917, the family expanded again with the birth of the fifth daughter, Edith Bolier, and in 1923, Donald Bolier, the second son was born.

In 1926-28, my Mother, Florence, attended the state Teachers College in River Falls, Wisconsin. She graduated in 1929 with a two-year certificate qualifying her for teaching in the lower grades. While a student at River Falls, she played competitive tennis, swam in competition and learned the Banjo/uke for its dormitory entertainment value. Since her mom was still not well, she shouldered much of the housekeeping projects at home on weekends.

In 1919-1933, federal law prohibited the manufacture, sale, and distribution of alcoholic beverages in the USA. Fred had a family of nine to support and a sick wife when he learned of a source of distilled spirits in South St Paul, Minnesota. He became a part-time dealer of illegal beverages to a very private list of Speak-Easy's and "Blind-Pigs" in St Croix County of Western Wisconsin. Many of these places were hidden away and cleverly disguised to avoid detection.

Prohibition was repealed in 1933. Fred Bolier was then appointed area distributor for Western Wisconsin for Miller High Life, Pabst Blue Ribbon and Walters, (The Beer that Is Beer from Eau Claire.) He already knew the customers from his bootleg days. They were the bars, nightclubs, resorts, hotels, "Blind Pigs and Speak-Easy's in his bootleg route book.

Fred was alert and resourceful in building new ventures. Upon the repeal of Prohibition in 1933, he built a collection of ventures to make any entrepreneur smile. In addition to distributing beer, he was active in building the Bolier Amusement Company, placing coin-operated amusement machines in business establishments on a co-op plan where he and the establishment owner shared in the revenue. Single-play Wurlitzer Juke Boxes holding over 150 78 RPM records, bumper pool games, pin-ball machines, bowling machines and shuffle-board machines were all a part of this business. He owned hundreds of slot machines and also placed these machines in bars, nightclubs, bus stations, resorts and taverns all over West Central Wisconsin from River Falls to New Richmond and east to Menomonie.

The Federal government outlawed slot machines in the early 1940's and Fred did his duty and disposed of all his slot machines. He also invested in farms and residential real estate during these days.

Following his service in WWII, Uncle Don came home to his family. Fred assisted him in purchasing a gas station in Farmington, Minnesota, a venture, which had a short life, and soon Don, Dorothy and two sons were back living in Baldwin with Don learning the ropes of Fred's businesses. Don learned to service the amusement games and would frequently be required to interrupt family events to go on a service call.

Chapter 2
ECONOMIC HARD TIMES AND WORLD WAR II

HARD TIMES IN THE 1930's

1929 was generally considered the beginning of The Great Depression with a disaster in the stock market and a collapse of the nation's banking system. At its depth, millions were out of work, banks had failed, losing the savings of their depositors, and soup kitchens were started wherever possible to feed some of the hungry people. CCC (Civilian Conservation Corps) and WPA (Works Progress Administration) were begun as US Government programs to put people to work on projects ranging from improving facilities in National parks to building new roads. It all helped but the US economy remained "in the tank".

Among many other types of casualties of the Great Depression, farmers were unable to meet the ongoing costs of farming, often abandoning equipment in the fields. It was also the situation of some of the pioneer families in the area north of St Croix Falls where the O'Neil's, and the Orr's had settled. The O'Neil homestead in Burnett County had been barely maintained by Uncle John O'Neil until the 1920's. Many properties of the area were forced into foreclosure by the banks and/or the County for unpaid taxes in the 1930's.

In 1933, a young man from St Croix Falls, WI was out of work and visiting his sister, Margaret (Peg) and brother-in-law Mike Heebink in Baldwin, Wisconsin. Peg and Mike had taken over the Heebink family dairy farm on the South edge of the village of Baldwin. Mike Heebink hired the brother–in-law to paint the barn and to assist on the farm. The brother-in-law was my dad, Francis Eugene O'Neil. Sr.

Later, in visiting the local shops in town, my dad noticed an attractive young brunette, Florence Bolier, daughter of the owner of the variety store. Apparently, the attraction was mutual. Within the year, they were married. (by a JP in Hudson Wisconsin, strange because the family was very Catholic) and they set up housekeeping in Baldwin near the Bolier home.

These were the tough times of the Great Depression. Prohibition was repealed in 1932 and Fred Bolier was appointed Distributor of Pabst, Miller Hi Life and Walters beers to the saloons and night-spots in western Wisconsin. He hired his new son-in-law to deliver the beer. My folks got a small apartment in Baldwin.

On March 2, 1935, I was born. The tiny village of Baldwin did not have a hospital, so my pregnant mother was taken to St. Croix, Falls, the home town of my dad, where the local doctor (Dr. Jake Riegel) was a family friend of the O'Neils. The birth took place in the Riegel home, a part of which was the local hospital in 1935.

In 1938, My dad had been offered a job delivering beer for the Walters family, owners of Walters, 'The Beer That Is Beer' of Eau Claire, Wisconsin. He left the job with father-in-law Fred Bolier and relocated our little family of three to Eau Claire.

EAU CLAIRE, WISCONSIN, MY HOME TOWN

Eau Claire, Wisconsin, was founded by French traders in the late 1700's. It is strategically located at the confluence of the Chippewa and Eau Claire Rivers in a large valley created by huge amounts of glacial melt water 10,000 years prior.

Because of its location on two south-flowing rivers, the city prospered during the 1800's and early 1900's when the White Pine forests covered most of Northern Wisconsin. Eau Claire was the center of the action for west central Wisconsin boasting of many sawmills on the shores of its rivers and on the remnants of an old meandering river horseshoe now named Half Moon Lake. Sawmills, their support network and railroads were Eau Claire's economic engines closely followed by agriculture.

Lumber camps in the wilderness would harvest virgin White Pine trees of white wood, straight grain and easily formed to suit the dreams of the architectural builders of the day. Logs would be floated down the rivers directly into the sawmills built on the shores of the rivers. The mills would saw the logs into dimension lumber and ship it to markets in Milwaukee, Chicago and throughout the mid-west.

The city of Eau Claire became home to many very wealthy families who erected stunning homes and businesses of Victorian architecture, some of which are restored and still stand as an elegant picture of the past. Eau Claire's downtown reflected similar tastes and preferences, however nearly all of these buildings were demolished and replaced by brick buildings with modern (and boring) geometry.

The city fathers supported and had the financial resources to bring comfort and class to the city. Streets and neighborhoods were well planned, streets were paved, streetcars were providing public transportation, early city parks and green space was well planned, and churches of many faiths with beginnings back in the mid 1800's were founded by the citizens. Elementary school wards were planned, separating the city into 10 wards, each school near the center of the neighborhood it served. A college was founded in 1916, and thousands of us have graduated from that school, now the University of Wisconsin, Eau Claire.

My first memories of Eau Claire are from our little apartment at 555 Erin Street. It was 1940, and I was five years old! We had one bedroom where all three of us slept, a small kitchen with an ice box (no refrigerator), a small living room with a wood/coal burning stove and a bathroom with tub and a kerosene-heater to heat the room. My big job around the house was to haul out the ashes from the stove and lug in a pail of coal for the stove.

My friends in the neighborhood were Billy Bonesho, age 6, Grace Sherwood, age 4, and Harold "Skeets" Lind, age 5. Bill and Grace are still my friends even after nearly 80 years. Grace lives in Watertown, South Dakota, Bill and his wife Carole live in Circle Pines Minnesota, just 2 miles from us in Shoreview. The Bill and Carole Bonesho family, have been like our family since.

Bill's dad, Mott Bonesho, and my dad, were high school classmates in St Croix Falls in the 1920's. Our dads each had two sisters who were also buddies in school in the 1920's. And to broaden the coincidence ... the Bonesho family relocated to Eau Claire about the same time in the 1930's as my family,

In 1942 – I recall an account of Billy Bonesho and me out shoveling snow off the Bonesho sidewalk. As usual, Billy was shoveling fast and the snow was flying off his shovel. He shoveled too close to me and his shovel struck me just to the left of my left eye. The fear in my folks was the possible infection from the wound migrating to the eye. The Doctor prescribed an awful tasting sulfa medication, which required I take a dose every few hours, 24 hours a day. I recall to this day fighting my parents with all my strength to avoid swallowing that bad stuff! I still give Bill hell for that one.

Later on, possibly when we were about eight years old, I was attending a Halloween party at the Bonesho neighbors. My mask had a full beard and at some stage of the party, I stepped out of the party and onto the porch to look at my pumpkin, which was lit with a candle! In an instant, the mask was ablaze with big flames in the beard, which had caught fire as I stooped over to peek. I was attempting to tear off the mask when my buddy, Bill Bonesho, saw me fumbling and dashed out to assist. He pulled the flaming mask off my face and I had only singed eyebrows resulting from the experience. I have thanked him often for that act of valor. The story hit the newspapers in Eau Claire and Minneapolis/St. Paul.

My folks were living on a very modest income. My dad was not well paid, and though my mother was trained and certified to teach, this was the "Great Depression." There were very few jobs and many people unemployed. Families were asked to not have two wage earners in the family because it may deprive another family from having even one member earning wages. I learned later my parents had moved to Eau Claire because Walters would pay my dad a little better than Grandpa.

After rent, food, clothing and utilities, there was not much left. We did not have a car, so my dad walked to work. We never traveled except to visit grandparents maybe twice annually when we caught the Greyhound Bus from Eau Claire to Baldwin, a trip of about 50 miles. And, because my parents had to borrow a bit of money to get married and set up housekeeping in 1933, they had lingering debt service. And, the "Sharks" of the day were not of a mind to be reasonable in applying interest to the borrowed funds.

I did not understand it all, but the Great Depression lasted until December, 1941, when the outbreak of WW II unlocked the economy and sent it firmly into recovery and expansion. Millions of Americans were put back to work. They flooded into military service, defense industries and thousands of other ways in support of US Allies working together to win.

SCHOOL DAYS

The Eau Claire school system in 1940 was divided into Wards, each with its own geographic area. Teachers were all women and most had obtained their teaching degree from the Eau Claire State Teachers College, our local four-year college with an excellent reputation. Ethnically speaking, the city was largely Norwegian and Lutheran, German and Catholic. There were two school systems, the Catholic schools and everyone else attended the Public Schools divided into 10 "Wards".

I completed Kindergarten at the 10th Ward school. First grade was to begin in early September, 1941, just after Labor Day. My first-grade teacher was Miss Kinnan, an experienced elementary teacher who was late for school that first week. After travel in Europe all summer, her planned return voyage from England had ended abruptly when her ship was sunk by a German U-Boat. The Zam-Zam was an Egyptian Freighter, and Germany had many submarines patrolling the North Atlantic with orders from Germany to torpedo any ship that appeared to carry freight.

There was no air travel for most people in those days of the early 1940's, so when foreign travel was in your plan, it always required travel by ocean vessel. Miss Kinnan returned to America and arrived at school just a few weeks late to begin the first grade for us. This event was my first awareness of war. I was just a first grader and my teacher was in it, making it personal. Little did a six-year-old know of war but that was about to change by December, 1941, just three months later.

I completed the second through the sixth grade at the Eighth Ward Elementary School in Eau Claire. Our country was at war, my Dad was away for two years at work on road construction in Canada. My uncles were in the military and stationed in places like the Panama Canal, England, France, North Africa, Italy, Belgium and eventually, Germany.

Elementary school days from 1942-1946 were largely without a Dad figure. My Mother and I were living in Eau Claire with no nearby family and no family automobile. At my Mothers urging I joined the YMCA and spent lots of time there. She taught me history and geography relating to the war we were in and did her best to get me exposed to other activities in scouting and Presbyterian Church activities for young people. I was active in the school patrol doing traffic control at corners near the school, neighborhood softball and casual after-supper games in the neighborhood.

From time to time the Billy Bonesho family of Billy, his Mom Mary, sister Janet and my Mother and I would walk to the shore of the Chippewa River just a few blocks from our respective homes for a time in the sand and enjoy a wiener roast. Billy's dad was also gone during those years serving in the US Navy. Then, their family moved to Spring Brook, Wisconsin to be near his Moms family. I did not see Billy again until 1952 for short visit when he was playing football for our local college team. We met up again in 1958 as married college students at UW Eau Claire and renewed our friendship now in its 7th decade.

THE WAR YEARS

I will never forget December 7, 1941. I have relived the day many times over, including in 1997, when Sandy and I visited the Pearl Harbor site of the Battleship Arizona on our 40th anniversary trip to Hawaii.

Skeets Lind and I, all of six years old, were on the living room floor of our house on Sunday afternoon, December 7 on Erin Street in Eau Claire "reading" the comics from the Sunday paper. The radio was on, and my Mother and Dad were in the room reading the paper as well. Skeets and I were jabbering, as two little boys are prone to do, when very suddenly, my dad asked us to "stop talking" in his most stern voice.

President Franklin D. Roosevelt was informing the world that the Japanese had bombed and destroyed US Navy and US Army Air Corps facilities, ships and aircraft in Pearl Harbor, Hawaiian Islands, that morning. "A day which will live in infamy" were his words. We declared war on Japan, the next day Germany declared war on the USA. Now it is all-out World War II on two fronts, the European Front and the Pacific Front. The "war to end all wars" had ended in 1918, just 25 years before, and the USA says "What happened?"

Within days, thousands of men, many unemployed or underemployed for months or years, were standing in lines to volunteer. Civilian readiness began quickly, even in Eau Claire, Wisconsin, located thousands of miles from the bad guys. Blackout curtains, air defense procedures, conservation of all resources began. Gasoline was virtually unavailable and rationed to about one gallon per week for civilians.

The Tire plant in Eau Claire switched quickly to military tires only, the "Presto" plant in Eau Claire known for its pressure cookers and other small kitchen appliances tooled up to produce artillery ammunition and small arms ammo. All kinds of metals, including steel, aluminum and copper plus rubber, oil and petroleum were to be recycled or preserved for the military. We even saved string, which had tied the small packages of meat from the market. We peeled the tinfoil off the gum wrapper to recycle. We recycled newspaper and magazines for recycled paper packaging of military products.

All of the U.S. automobile manufacturing and general manufacturing was converted to the building of tanks, trucks, aircraft, ships, guns and ammunition. Mills and fabric production were converted to the war effort making clothing and supplies for the military, thousands and thousands of parachutes for example. Hundreds of thousands of uniforms and footwear were going to be needed very soon. Medical supplies and medical equipment producers went into round-the-clock production.

Uncles Bernard (Red) Norwick, Don Bolier, Roy (Speck) Nelson and Paul Norelius went to war in the US Army. (Fortunately, all returned.) War bonds were being sold everywhere to finance the war effort. Every school child in the country was asked to contribute by buying War Bonds and War Stamps. A War bond for which we paid $18.75 would be worth $25.00 in ten years. Each week we would go to school with one or two dimes to buy some stamps for our war bond.

THE ROAD TO ALASKA

The Japanese were on a roll. Their Navy, Air Forces and Army were well supplied with equipment and man-power. Their military rolled through the South Pacific invading China and occupying many Islands of the South Pacific, including the last island in the chain of the Aleutian Islands, which are possessions of the United States of America. The Aleutian chain is a part of Alaska, and the chain is the last visible part of a long-ago mountain range spread out southwest of Alaska in the Pacific leading towards Japan.

Military Strategists agreed that since the proximity of the string of the Aleutian Islands lead directly to North America through Alaska, that the U.S. had better prepare a plan to get an army to Alaska if necessary. Since Japan had already occupied the last island in the chain, it was speculated that Japan was telegraphing their intention to invade North America by land! By sea, their task was thousands of miles … by land, only hundreds.

In 1942, the US Army Corps of Engineers, (the US Army construction company) began a road-building project of dramatic proportions. Beginning in Dawson Creek, BC, Canada, the construction of a highway-to-Alaska began. The early accounts are sobering. Surveyors entered the woods, made axe cuts on trees to define the max width of the roadway, followed immediately by bull dozers to knock down the trees, pull the stumps, followed by graders and thousands of truckloads of rock and gravel, followed by culvert installers and bridge builders. Through the perma-frost, the mountainous passes and swamps, fighting mosquitoes "as big as sparrows" and in minus 50-degree-below-zero weather they advanced.

In an amazing twelve months, there was a road to Alaska. They call it the ALCAN ... even today. It was a twelve-hundred-mile dirt road until recent years... but it was a road – even though many hazards needed improvements. In 1943, civilian U.S. Road Construction Contractors were contracted to improve the road. Straightening and removing big curves, reinforcing bridges, placing larger culverts under the road where large amounts of storm water passed through, improving the surfaces by spreading tens of thousands of yards of gravel on the road beds to improve the surfaces were some of the projects scheduled.

My dad was working for Walters in Eau Claire and continued to receive low wages. He learned of the big Canadian road construction project. The money was better than twice his Wisconsin earnings. As a safe driver with lots of hours in trucks, he qualified for the work, and he was not likely to be drafted into the Army because of his age. He and my mother agreed that they could sacrifice this way, get out of debt, and begin a nest-egg to buy a house when the war was over. The trade-offs were clear to both of them.

It was just about like enlisting in the military, except his four brothers-in-law were in the Army for an undetermined period of time, and he was assured his contract was limited to nine months. And, nobody would be shooting at him. His contract would require working long hours in harsh weather conditions. During the summer months when the sun was shining 18 hours a day, they worked many hours. Days were shorter in the dead of winter when the temperature often fell to -30 to -40 and sometimes -50 degrees below zero. They were advised to bring their warmest clothing. My Dad had union suits underwear made of heavy 100 percent virgin wool. He layered with wool shirts, heavy sox and good boots, chopper mitts and a wool hat with thick ear flaps.

The construction workers were transported by rail from their homes, mostly from the upper Midwest, to Seattle then north into British Columbia a few hundred miles, then to Dawson Creek, British Columbia, in trucks and old busses several hundred miles further north. They slept in Army tents heated with small stoves and in US Army sleeping bags. They ate in US Army mess halls. There was little time for anything but work. The Japanese military continued to occupy more and more territory in the Pacific, and the USA was unprotected from the north. Roadwork was high priority. His 9-month contract ended in late 1943, and he came home to Wisconsin. We were so happy to see him.

My mother had been a champion while he was gone. With my Dad gone she would coach me on the maps and geography of the war zones and where the war was being fought. She taught me about the geography of Canada. She would make a big batch of buttered popcorn for snacks (I still love it). She would take me and my fish pole on the city bus to Lake Hallie where we would rent a boat for a few hours and I could fish, we would walk to a nearby store for an ice cream cone, and once in a great while we would walk several blocks to the Eau Claire Café for their Blue-Plate Special ... roast beef, mashed potatoes and gravy over two slices of bread at 50 cents a plate.

There were fewer cars on the streets, more homes flying small pennants in their windows with blue stars representing the number of boys from that family serving in the military. Gold stars represented the family member had been killed in action. Butter, sugar, gasoline, and a hundred other commodities were rationed. My mother had a small booklet, each page of which was filled with little stamps entitling her to purchase one pound of butter each month, one 5# sack of flour, and so on.

Every newspaper, and especially on Sunday, always had a big spread of the maps of the European theater and another of the South Pacific placing the U.S. and the enemy forces. The paper became an incredible source of geography training for a third and fourth grader. I recall very distinctly when the American forces, led by General MacArthur returned to the Island of Luzon, in the Philippines. I knew where the Philippines were located on the map and I was thrilled with myself. My mother was mostly responsible for my awareness of the geography of Central Europe and the vast Pacific.

My Dad had a great appreciation for the potential of a national emergency. And when he returned from Canada, after his nine-month contract had been completed four of his brothers-in-law were in the military and overseas... and the road to Alaska was not yet complete. It was obvious the country was at war. Trainloads of trucks, tanks, big artillery guns and personnel carriers were on the Chicago/Northwestern RR tracks cruising through Eau Claire. They were en-route from manufacturers throughout the mid-west to West Coast Ports and then to the Pacific Theater.

The Gillette Tire and Rubber Co, a major industry in Eau Claire was shipping thousands of tires to the military, and Presto Industries, another large Eau Claire Co., famous for Pressure cookers and other small kitchen appliances was making munitions.

It was 1944, my Dad had been home for a few weeks to a country at war in other lands. The road in Canada was not done ... so he re-upped and signed another contract. He went back to remote Canada with another nine-month commitment.

Cities and locations, we had never heard of were on the list of return addresses from his mail. Dawson Creek, BC; Ft. St John, BC; Ft. Nelson, BC; Summit Lake, BC; Watson Lake in the Yukon, and after the Pelly Mountains and many months later came Whitehorse, Yukon Territories.

In letters home to my mother and me he related some of the work he was doing. Many of the bridges built by the Army Engineers in 1942 were suspect because the weight of the newest Army equipment was heavier now requiring a strengthening. Some of the culverts placed to allow runoff to flow beneath the bridges required doubling up to prevent washouts.

In one harrowing episode, he was hauling a large and very heavy bulldozer across the mountain 40 miles to another site where it was needed. The Dozer was loaded onto a large, heavy flat-bed truck. The Diesel-powered rigs used by the construction people were never allowed to be shut off in the winter months because the fuel would 'Gel'. The haul left its location, as he described it, "snorting." Big Diesel truck hauling big Bulldozer with engine running. The haul was over a mountain on a narrow road with no safety fencing … and a 1200-foot drop.

In 1944, when his second contract ended, he came home to stay. The good news is the road was never needed to support the relocation of an Army to defend our northern borders. It has since been used by thousands of tourists traveling to Alaska. For many years it was 1200 miles of dirt and gravel. Those who ventured were aware that gas tanks often became punctured on the journey, so steel shields covering the gas tanks were essential. Bringing along a spare windshield was recommended, nose cones protecting car hoods, spare tires, bumpers, radiators, headlights and fenders were essential.

Home again, my dad landed a job right away selling road

construction machinery for a firm in Southern Minnesota. Unfortunately, the manufacturers were still producing military equipment and bull-dozers, graders, compactors and other equipment was not in post-war production for at least two years.

Fortunately, the Walters people liked him well enough to promote him to a Field Sales Position. He got a raise, a company car, he wore a suit and tie every day and things began to look up for my parents.

THE WAR GOES ON

Throughout the two-year period of 1943 and 44, my mother was a single parent and I was not a model child. I had energy for doing boy stuff and she knew girl stuff best because of her duties as surrogate mom for her four sisters when her Mom was sick. Still, she was very influential in my life. She knew little about baseball and basketball but had been in competitive sports in college playing tennis, and swimming.

She became a Den Mother when I started in Cub Scouts at age 9, and she encouraged me to join Boy Scouts when I was 12. She encouraged me to join the YMCA and get involved in organized sports. I discovered basketball and enjoyed the sport for many years. There was no little league, or city sponsored youth sports programs in Eau Claire in the 40's, but the "Y" was very active and developed many great athletes in the city.

I took charge of recruiting a basketball team for the "B" league, the 8-year-old's league, from among my friends at the "Y". There were about seven of us, and we knew very little about the game except that the ball went into the basket, and only five of us could play at one time. The others were subs. We received a bit of coaching from one of the older boys at the Y. He was maybe age 11 at the time. He and a fellow working for the "Y" helped us over the bare essentials the first year. Other teams in the "B" league were as unskilled as we were, and the floor was peppered with little boys running all about hollering for the ball.

The games were maybe 30 minutes long, and the B league teams played all their games early on Saturday, so it was common for the entire team to hang around to watch the older boys play as the day progressed into late afternoon when the 15-17 year-old boys played.

I developed a system of charting and graphing players and scoring etc. in that first year. We 8-year-olds playing basketball ordered matching colored shirts so we were more likely to pass the ball to a teammate when appropriate. It may be the reason the boys asked me to do it every year thereafter. That system of charting, which came quite naturally to me has been a technique I have used and adapted in dozens of situations since. All through my Air Force, college, work for several companies and my self-employment and entrepreneurial days, I have used the technique or a variation on it. Even today at age 83, I use the system to chart my blood pressure. It is now known as a spread-sheet.

My mother attended many of my basketball games at the Y, and I was always happy when she came to watch. She was very happy when I completed the learn-to-swim class at the Y. She was encouraging me to get into the Y after-school program where, following some vigorous play in the gym, everybody hit the pool.

She taught me to respect women – opening the door for a lady and walking on the outside closest to the curb/street. She taught me how to set a table and proper placement of the knife, fork and spoon. She taught me how to make a bed with hospital corners, a skill that came in handy just a few years later when I was in the Air Force. She taught cleanliness of the person, the house and the surroundings. She always scraped up the dollars to send me to YMCA summer camp at Camp Manitou near New Auburn, Wisconsin. Camp was my favorite part of summer vacation.

She taught me geography. During the war when every Sunday paper would have the full-page maps of the war zones, the location of the Allied Forces and the German or Japanese military forces, she would teach.

She taught me thrift. "Save a dime today and put it towards a war bond, which will earn interest." "Put your money in the bank but don't trust everything to one bank, remember many banks failed in the Depression." Her favorite saying about thrift was "a penny saved is a penny earned". As a single mom she earned an "A" and I will remember her guidelines forever.

During those war years of 1943 and 44, I began my first business venture. Paper for recycling was in great demand for the war effort. I was motivated by the war effort, the shortage of money from home and a new baseball glove I saw in the local sports shop.

I discovered a salvage business within a few blocks of my neighborhood. They were big recyclers of iron, steel, brass, copper and aluminum and had a steady stream of trucks bringing in old steel farm machinery salvaged from the hills, fields, private dumping grounds, and wherever else they could find the stuff. Later, I realized that during the depression farmers who were unable to stay afloat would sell their stuff if possible, if not, they would abandon old equipment in the fields and sheds and their homes to head for town, for Milwaukee, or for California.

My venture was worth a few dollars a month for me. I was knocking on doors in our neighborhood asking for the contribution of old newspapers, magazines, boxes and cartons to recycle for the war effort. Most were happy to unload their used paper products. I would load it on my wagon and haul it to the salvage yard receiving 2 cents per pound for my effort. Often, I would collect over 100 pounds and come away with $2. I bought a new baseball glove (which I still own) a fishing pole and other stuff an 8 or 9-year-old boy needed.

One time, the Phillips family, a local family connected to the recycling firm, let the word out that everyone who collected 500 pounds of paper during a several week period would be rewarded with a free trip to Minneapolis to attend a football game – Minnesota playing Nebraska at Memorial Stadium on campus. Now this was a big deal for an 8-year-old who had never been more than 50 miles away from home. I joined about 25 others for the award trip, which included $1 for treats and free lunch.

It was a thrill I have never forgotten and all because of the generosity of the Louis Phillips family of Eau Claire. The trip was memorable even today – 75 years later. A bus ride, a big football game in a big stadium with thousands of fans and a marching band. Cool stuff for a nine-year-old from a very modest family situation.

The Phillips family also donated a large tract of forestland with lakes near Haugen, (Rice Lake area) Wisconsin, where my friends and I went to Scout camp in the late 1940's. This is Camp Phillips, pride of The Boy Scouts from Eau Claire. The same family that donated a large amount of money to the University of Wisconsin, Eau Claire, for a science building in about 1960. A very generous family.

My four Uncles were in the war. Uncle Don Bolier drove an ambulance in the war zones of Europe. Uncle Roy (Speck) Nelson was in Panama, virtually always on alert to a sudden enemy attempt to take over or damage the Canal – a vital link between the Atlantic and Pacific Oceans. Uncle Paul Norelius was in the infantry in Europe. Uncle (Red) Bernard Norwick was in the North Africa Desert Campaign opposing the insane German Tank Corps and the Desert Fox, then Sicily, then Belgium and Germany. He was decorated with the Bronze Star and the Silver Star and two Purple Hearts before it was all done. I still have his medals.

In 1945, at the close of the war, Uncle Red had the honor of being in the squad that accepted the personal sidearm pistols being surrendered by three of the most notorious and cruel German Generals; Goering, Von Rundstedt and Kesselring. All were tried at the Nurnberg War Trials and all were bad-asses.

My Uncle Myron (Mike) Heebink and Aunt Margaret (Peg) operated a family dairy farm on the outskirts of Baldwin, Wisconsin. In today's language of business, they were a "Vertically Integrated Farming Enterprise." Their cows grazed on-site, were milked by the family, milk cooled in 10-gallon cans in very cold water in the milk-house, the family bottled the milk and cream, and Uncle Mike, with his trusty horse, "Pete," delivered the bottled milk door-to-door from his horse drawn milk cart. And, Pete knew every stop on the route!

Aunt Peg was Lady-in-Charge-of-Kitchen. Always had good things to eat. And then, she would take me out to the chicken coop to gather eggs. I think the chickens loved her and hated me.

Uncle Mike was too old to serve in the military, but Aunt Peg contributed to the war effort in other ways. Through their church, she "adopted" a needy Dutch family in occupied Holland. She regularly sent them clothes, personal items and home-canned food. She also regularly contributed home-canned food and other items to be included in Care Packages sent to the military serving on the "front."

THE WAR ENDS

The war was over in 1945, and things began to return to normal. My uncles, thankfully returned from the war. My dad was back from two years in Canada and Alaska. Things were better now. We had a company car to use for the family on weekends. We could take a one-week vacation at a lake near Cameron, Wisconsin. And, we could go to Baldwin and St Croix Falls to see cousins, aunts, uncles and grandparents more often. My dad taught me to drive, fish, ride a bike, use hand-tools, shoot a rifle, how to bowl and how to make a great sling-shot.

I signed up for a paper route and began delivering 27 Milwaukee Sentinel newspapers every weekday morning and 100 on Sunday. I now began to understand the responsibilities of the merchant (me the carrier) and the customer in a business transaction.

My folks were finally able to pay off the old loans left over from the depression, purchase our first refrigerator and throw out the old ice-box, purchase a new sofa and throw out the old broken-down sofa which had been in our houses since 1934. And, we rented a home with central heating – no more space heater in the living room.

As peacetime evolved, more goods became available to everyone. I specifically recall seeing my first ball-point pen. Also, the first new car since 1941, though the cars were delivered with wood planks in place of front and rear bumpers. When steel bumpers became available the wood was replaced. I was asked by my mother to walk the six blocks to a drug store near our home where the rumor was that Kleenex would be available for the first time in several years.

Products manufactured in Japan from scrap metals from the war began to flood the toy departments at stores. Small vehicles, miniature boats and farm buildings made from salvaged food containers were showing up on the shelves. Soon the imports from Japan became known as "cheap Japanese crap". Not long thereafter, Japan began producing the high-tech they are so expert at today.

Army/Navy surplus stores filled with new and used military goods were a significant new type of retailer. From wearing apparel to mess kits and gas masks it was available in the many surplus stores to pop up in 1946 and 47. Then the stores evolved and began to get access to military duds of the enemy forces. Heavy duty wool pants and shirts from the Russian and Polish army surplus network would show up on the shelves.

Chapter 3
LIFE POST WAR

BETTER DAYS "A-COMIN"

After the war ended in 1945, big things began to happen. During the depression and war, the appetites of the public were never satisfied only suppressed. New homes, cars, furniture, education, marriage, children, business formations and in hundreds of other ways life's needs and wants were becoming possible.

My Dad was home from Canada and had a new job with Walters responsible for advertising, promotion and spreading good-will for the brand. Today we might name this position Sales Manager. He was provided a new car, traveled extensively throughout the Central Northwest area of Wisconsin. Walter's Beer-that-is-Beer would be considered a "craft beer" today, brewed in relatively small batches in a variety of seasonal flavors. In addition to the basic everyday product they made holiday brew, summer picnic brew, Bock Beer, a heavier product somewhat like a "Porter" which were all offered and were brewed under the close supervision of an attending "Brew Master."

My folks, who married in 1933, in the heart of the Great

Depression, had "done without." Now at the end of the war and the depression in 1945-6, in my little family a new sofa, a refrigerator, an apartment with central heating, a week' vacation at a lake became possible. My parents longed for a home of their own, on or near a lake. It was a big dream and a garage and a garden for my dad to putter in was very dreamy stuff.

In 1951 my parents finally became homeowners. They bought an older home with a wraparound porch overlooking Half Moon Lake, just a block from Luther Hospital where my Mother had a job she loved. This was their home until my Dad died in 1975 and my mother sold the place to the nearby growing Luther Hospital about 1985.

The sun began to shine on my parents. They could invite the families of the Boliers and the O'Neils and other friends to their house on Half Moon Lake for Sunday dinners, Thanksgiving, Easter, and birthdays. My Mother was a good cook and loved having them all come to her house for a change. In the summer she would take the kids down to the Half Moon Lake municipal beach just 2 blocks walk and coach them in the specifics of learn-to-swim.

In 1946, I entered the 6th grade at the 8th Ward school in Eau Claire. I was selected by teachers to become a Bike Cop. The city Police Department had developed a new program to encourage bike safety by using kids on bikes to do so. We were issued police badges, blue shirts and blue hats to wear, and we were given the power to hand out citations.

In the 6th grade I had a geography project to construct a map of South America using some concoction of flour, water, salt etc. on poster board. I carefully outlined the countries and built little mounds and pointy things to show the Andes Mountains. Just a few years ago, Sandy and I traveled to South America on a cruise the length of Chile, and only then did I realize how big those mountains are.

My 7th and 8th grades (1947 and 48) were pretty ordinary. Between school, the YMCA, Scouting, pick-up softball games, basketball leagues at the Y, and paper routes, my schedule was always full.

Through scouting I met some new friends who became a part of my life for more than 60 years. I joined the Scouts at the First Lutheran Church in Eau Claire and formed friendships with George Losby and Tom Hanson, both members of that church and that troop. George's Dad was a prominent Attorney and Tom's Dad was manager of a large department store. We clicked and were going to the same High School, lived in the same area of town so the friendships were cemented there and at summer scout camp and school activities.

George always had access to a car after we turned 16 and we began dating about the same time so "Double-Dating" meant he had access to the car. George was dating Sharon Kelly, and I had begun to date Sandy Tietge. We went to an occasional movie or an evening school event and deepened our friendship as couples leading to two big statements of friendship by George and me. One; <u>to be buddies to the end</u> (BTTE) and Two: <u>to be each other's Best Man</u>. We achieved both.

George enjoyed fishing and his family owned a cabin deep in the woods of Northern Wisconsin on the East Fork of the Chippewa River. There were Muskies in this river and we went to fish them. He borrowed a family car, we packed up our gear and headed for remote Winter, Wisconsin. I caught one Musky.

Because this trip was near Spring Brook, Wisconsin, the home of my old friend Billy Bonesho, we stopped to see the Bonesho family. Our visit was brief but fun to see this family with so many connections to the O'Neils over the years.

My dad had enjoyed bowling since he was young, and I had an interest in learning how to bowl. We would go to a local bowling alley in downtown Eau Claire named "The State Alleys." He would coach me in fitting the ball properly, throwing properly, where to aim to pick up "splits" and how to score properly. I was naturally well coordinated, and that was an asset in bowling. I bowled in leagues from age 16 until I was over 70. My biggest thrill was bowling a 175 average for a few years and a high game of 666.

HIGH SCHOOL DAYS

In 1949, I entered Eau Claire Senior High School as a Freshman in 9th grade. I made lots of new lifetime friends including Jim Nichols, Clayton Nibaur, Ben Ludowise, Ron Schlewitz and others. I took a straight class load, which included semesters in woodworking, metalworking, printing and mechanical drawing, plus math, English, history and biology.

The high school in Eau Claire was one full block square, in four stories, housing over 1600 students in four grades. There were roughly 50 class rooms and labs, a basketball floor with bleachers, a large auditorium with seating for several hundred, a large band room, other assorted rooms for administration and teacher lounges, plus a cafeteria.

The school had a good reputation for producing college-ready young people headed for institutions throughout the mid-west. Its athletic program was well known particularly in basketball and was a frequent entrée into the State High School tournament held at the University in Madison. The music program was well regarded, and the debate program was tops in the state.

My athletic love was for basketball, and I had played the game since second grade in the YMCA program. My goal was to be chosen to play for the high school varsity. Three years I tried and in the third year was chosen for the Jr. Varsity, but in the senior year of 1953 I failed to make the cut. Several of my friends were also disappointed.

It was then that we joined together into a team to play the game we loved at a little lower level. Jim Nichols, Jim Scolman, Ron Schlewitz, Bob Lorentz and Jet Johnson were on the team. We became the "Alley Trotters" and the Nicotine Five, though none of us were smokers. This team won the intramural league championship at school, the senior men's league championship at the YMCA, and we played and generally won over town teams from nearby communities. All in all, we played and had some fun and joy in our winning schedule. The varsity team won third at the state tournament in 1953, they deserved it and all were still friends.

During High School, I joined the De Molay, a Fraternal youth program sponsored by the Masonic Lodge. A number of my friends were involved and all were good people. My Dad had become a Mason, his Dad Charlie had been a Mason. The Eau Claire De Molay had a bowling team, I joined, and we held our own in a league where everyone else was older. They tolerated us young fellows and we became quite competitive playing against older and more experienced bowlers.

At age 16 I became eligible to be a blood donor. The

Bloodmobile visited the Masonic Temple several times a year. My Dad had been donating blood for some time so I tried it and found it comforting to learn someone, somewhere would receive my blood to help in their medical procedure. I have been donating blood since 1950 and have donated roughly 80 pints, or 5 gallons of whole Type B-Negative, thus far.

There was a favorite hamburger restaurant on Bellinger Street in Eau Claire named Ptomaine Tommy's! We, and many others from our age group would go there for a good burger and coke. Generally, we would double date with another couple having a family car to drive.

A "Hit" was staged at Ptomaine Tommy's. Tommy's was the scene of a faux murder in 1953. One dark and dreary night, my friend "Ade" Losby had borrowed the car from his brother and "borrowed" a .22 cal. pistol and some blank cartridges from his dad's gun collection. Another friend, "Frankie" Metz, joined us for the evening. Metz was going to take the hit! We let "Frankie" out of the car, he went into Tommy's grabbed a coke and sat down facing the front door.

We drove around for five minutes then "Ade" quietly eased the car up to the curb in front of Ptomaine Tommy's. "Jule" O'Neil, the "hit man," got out of the car, walked to the door of the restaurant, opened the door slightly and discharged the pistol inside the restaurant with three quick shots, then quickly back into the car, "Ade", gunned it to clear the area. The last view of the restaurant was seeing the proprietor, Bea Thompson (former Sheriff of Eau Claire County), out the door and onto the curb only to see the car disappear.

Later, at a pre-arranged place, we picked up "Frankie" and got the rest of the story from him. Frankie had slumped to the floor with great dramatics. Thompson was startled of course, as Frankie was picking himself up from the floor where he had feigned falling. The quick-thinking "Frankie" reported to Thompson "Oh, somebody had firecrackers."

There was another couple in the room when "Frankie" took the hit. I have often wondered how those people reported the event to their friends. Both "Ade" and "Frankie" are gone, so I am last to tell the story.

In 1950, as we were entering our second year of high school, war broke out in Korea and the United States got involved "to stop the threat of Communism." All my friends had experiences with family members who had served in the second world war of 1941-1945. We all realized we were soon to be of the age when the draft and military service would be required of us. At the very least, we would be required to serve time in the military, and at the worst, we would be required to serve in war zones.

We hoped for the best and began our sophomore year. I met some more lifetime friends – Bob Neperud and Jim Scolman, and renewed my old friendship with Grace Sherwood, my friend from the old Erin Street days. Sharon Kelly was dating my buddy George.

I had been attending Youth Fellowship group meetings at the North Presbyterian Church in Eau Claire but decided to change to the First Presbyterian Church group because more of my high school friends attended there.

I stopped delivering papers and started working at Hollen's Clothing, retailer of men's/women's clothing on North Barstow Street in Eau Claire. The store was managed by Joel Benyas, a friend of my dad. My job was to go in after school, receive and unpack new merchandise, count it in and matched to the shipping papers. I emptied all trash, removed ashes and clinkers from the furnace and hauled them out, filled the stoker with coal for the next day, dusted boxes, restocked shelves, and swept all wood floors with a compound of saw dust impregnated with oil. My wages were 45 cents per hour. Then, about one year later, the boss asked me to begin to work the sales floor. So, added to my duties was selling men's sport shirts, work boots, outer wear, Lee coveralls, gloves and mitts. I got a raise of 10%, or 5 cents an hour to 50 cents per hour.

In 1952, the Korean war was ongoing, and the military draft was active in taking young men for service at the ages of 19 or 20. The futures of all of us were uncertain, but surely would involve us in some Military Service. The new-found friendships with high school pals were often laced with talk of possible military service, sports, girls, hunting/fishing, classes in Physics, Math and English, recent movies starring Doris Day or John Wayne, the music of Frankie Laine, or Debbie Reynolds, hot new cars like the 49 Ford, Chev or the big Lincoln Continental.

SANDRA LOU TIETGE – THE GIRL THAT I MARRY

In January 1952, the Harold Tietge family relocated to Eau Claire from Sioux Falls, South Dakota. They were good Presbyterians and just arriving in the new city on Saturday, visited the First Presbyterian Church of Eau Claire on Sunday morning. It just happened to be Youth Sunday and the high school youth of the church were leading the morning service. I was involved in a reading or two. That Sunday evening, the youth of the church met for dinner as was customary. Obviously, much of the conversation was in discussing the morning service and the performance of our group of Senior Highs who participated.

My friend, Pete mentioned that the oldest daughter of a new visiting family was planning to attend our meeting that evening. She and the pastor's daughter arrived and they each joined right in to the conversation of the group. She was pretty, a bit timid, smart and friendly. I told my parents that night about the new girl who came to the meeting.

I believe I was "Smitten". Two days later, on Tuesday, I intentionally intercepted her en-route to her homeroom, and after greetings, I asked if she would attend the big basketball game that next Friday night with me. She said yes and I was very happy. Prior to this event, I had casually dated just a few times. I had not even thought ahead as to how I would transport her from her home to the high school gym and then back home. I was so incredibly naïve and uncomfortable, but so driven.

As it turned out, it didn't matter because on Thursday I had to call to advise her I had come down with the measles and had to break the date. A big embarrassment for me, but she understood. A Measles epidemic was running fast through our school. There were people at the game breaking out with the rash and many of the students were already out sick.

I collected my thoughts and courage and met her at the homeroom door many days later after I had returned to school. No apology was necessary, but I felt better and she said she understood after being in the school for a week and learning how widespread the disease was. She did attend the game with a group of new girls she had just met, and some of those girls have been friends for life.

For the rest of the story: Sandra's Dad Harold was degreed at

Iowa State, Ames, in Dairy Technology. He had been managing a large dairy products operation in Sioux Falls, South Dakota, and was the new manager of the Dolly Madison Milk and Ice Cream plants in Eau Claire. Cozette (Cozy) was trained as a teacher, but with four children, she now concentrated on being a great homemaker. The family included Sandra 15, Mike 11, Dennis 6 and Cheryl 2.

Assisting the family in the move were Charles and Mary Ellen Miller, Cozy's brother and his wife from St Paul. It was Mary Ellen who recommended to Sandra that going to the Senior High Fellowship Meeting on the first Sunday night might be a good way to meet and make friends with other young people from her new school.

I recall being very proud she was my date for the Junior prom in 1952. We still did not have a family automobile other than the company car my Dad drove. The company car was off-limits to a family member except when my dad was also in the car. But, Uncle Don Bolier, my mother's younger brother, to the rescue. He knew the predicament I was in and very generously drove his car over from Baldwin, gave me the keys and spent the evening with my parents. In the meantime, I drove over to pick up Sandy in a new Oldsmobile, then to the prom and following the prom to a soda fountain. Guess who was riding high??

We would date infrequently and generally walk where we were going or double date with one of our friends who had access to a car. Two things I could count on when dating Sandy. The first was when we got home to her house and opened the front door, a little music box attached to the door would ding away alerting Cozy and Harold we had returned, discouraging smooching on the sofa. The second was they always served us cheese and crackers or Ice cream at that time. When it was time for me to go home, I would walk or catch a bus. The distance was a bit over a mile.

FINALLY, A SENIOR

1953, the year I graduated from high school, was exciting but loaded with uncertainty. My mother had been urging me to plan for college for many years, but I was not a particularly good student and academically felt unsuited for college at this time. Besides, I had no notion of a career path to prepare for, unlike some of my friends who knew they wanted to teach, become an engineer, practice medicine or law, I was stuck in a rut of indecision.

To complicate matters, we were still involved in a shooting war in Korea, and the War Department had an efficient Selective Service function, which guaranteed to supply thousands of new recruits for military service each month. All young men of draft age were classified for future military service and assigned a number for the draft lottery. After high school, each of us became eligible for the draft.

During the year, Sandy and I had dated a few times and become better acquainted. She accepted my invitation to go to the Holiday Ball, which was held every year on the day following Christmas. This was as big as it gets in Eau Claire in the early 1950's, and it had a history going back many years to the "Big Band "era of the 1920's and 30's. It was a formal affair; the band was Jimmy Dorsey (Bro of Tommy) and it was an elegant event. Again, Uncle Don generously shared his car.

Later, in 1953, Sandy and I were a couple at the Senior prom. I rode up again on my Uncle Don's white horse and whisked away Sandy to the Ball feeling smug and very happy. We would dance, go to a late dinner then home. When I arrived, Uncle Don would then head back home.

In June 1953, I was graduating from high School and the Korean war truce was signed in the same month. I was still dating Sandy. I had been a part of a winning basketball team, the Alley Trotters, and had quit my job at Hollens to go out for track. I ran my best half-mile in 2.05 minutes, found a new job at a commercial bakery at more than twice my prior wage rate, saved my money and bought my first car (1942 Chevrolet for $150). This car was one of the last produced by General Motors before switching over to military vehicles in 1942. I registered for trade school at Eau Claire Vo-Tec in the HVAC area.

The Korean Truce did not mean an end to the draft, but it did mean when we went into the service, we could take some comfort that nobody would be shooting at us.

Following graduation in June, several of my friends and I formed an informal clan. "Boys run in packs" was the statement by some. I was a non-drinker, so I became the unofficial Designated Driver. We all had jobs, so nights and weekends were our times to roam. We played basketball in-doors and out on school grounds, visited a local soda fountain for a malt and a game of hearts, and we visited the nearby county fairs in Chippewa Falls, Colfax and Mondovi. We ended many evenings at The Hoot, a local beer bar just outside the Eau Claire city and county limits. The Hoot was a nightclub with a juke-box, a dance floor and became a hang-out for teens from all over the area.

As the Non-Drinking Designated Driver, I watched over my boys and made sure they got home safely and successfully – until one night when two of the boys and their dates were driving on a winding dirt road and the driver missed a turn and crashed into a tree. Ron, the other guy in the back seat went through the windshield and was blind in one eye for the rest of his life.

Nobody said it, but everybody knew it, this would be our last few weeks of hanging out with the guys. Jim Scolman left for California to work in the aircraft industry, two more enlisted in the military, I started school in September and worked at night. My friend Nep (Bob Neperud) had graduated in the class of 1952 and was working at Dolly Madison Dairy, indirectly for Sandy's dad.

Sandy and I continued casual dating. She was a Senior and had decided to go to nursing school in Minneapolis after graduation. She would begin at Abbott Hospital School of Nursing, an intensive 36 straight months of training in all the academic subjects, as well as substantial on the "Floor" hands-on nursing procedures and practices.

Chapter 4
THE AIR FORCE, MARRIAGE AND BEYOND

ENLISTING IN THE USAF

In early 1954, Nep confided in me that he was going to enlist in the military to avoid being drafted into the Army Infantry. Because he was a year older than me, his lottery number was coming up soon. My second semester at sheet metal school was going along ok, but it did not hold the promise for a satisfying lifetime vocation, so I agreed to enlist with him. We chose the U.S. Air Force. The enlistment was a minimum of four years where, if drafted into the army, the minimum was just three years. We agreed, four years in the Air Force was better than three in the infantry.

The Air Force has many career tracks to professional and semi-professional civilian occupations one could seek out after completing the four-year military tour. Further, we would be eligible for a full basket of GI Bill benefits as awarded to the vets of the Korean War, including a monthly salary while attending school. The monthly amount increased if married and again with children. There were GI Mortgage benefits when buying a house, and medical benefits for life, if needed, through the VA.

We informed our families, and the next day we visited the Air Force Recruiter in Eau Claire. He was a classy dude and looked great in his dress blues. One week later we were on our way to Minneapolis for testing, physicals and swearing in.

In the few days before leaving for Minneapolis, I asked Sandy to go on a little trip with me for the day. We visited my Grandparents Maggie and Charlie in St. Croix Falls, Wisconsin, and my Aunt Carol, Uncle Paul and cousins Neil and Jay Norelius in Lindstrom, Minnesota. Getting home after dinner, we said our good-byes and promised "we'll write".

Nep and I were sworn into the U.S. Air Force on March 31, 1954. Within two hours, we and four other fellows from Minnesota, including Ron Anderson of Walnut Grove, were on a train to our basic training base at Lackland AF Base in San Antonio, Texas. This was my first experience out of Wisconsin and Minnesota.

In San Antonio, at 7AM of the third day, we were met by a blue Air Force Bus and transported to the base for our first GI breakfast, a treat they called SOS. SOS, we learned was creamed hamburger on toast. Nick-named by GI's long before us, SOS was Shit-on-a-Shingle.

There was a total of 60 of us leaving that mess hall under the guidance of a Sgt Haugen that morning. Sgt Haugen was a sharply dressed, buttoned down, all-business character with three stripes on his sleeve and sharp creases in his shirt and trousers. He had 60 new recruits dressed in multi-colored civilian duds looking like a rainbow to march (walk) about a mile to where our barracks was located. And, as our "Mother and Father" for the next 12 weeks, he was going to make us "Airmen!" We had black, white and tan faces, hair cut styles ranging from cleanly tapered around the ears to wads of hair on the back of the head which at the time was called a Duck's-Ass.

The motley group arrived at the barracks, which was to be our home for the next 11 weeks. There must have been 500 of these identical buildings on this base of tens of thousands of Airmen. The building was a two-story, wood structure with both floors having double bunks stretching the full length of the building with a center aisle. Each of us were assigned a foot locker at the end of our bed, and we learned quickly how to organize it properly to hold all our stuff. The showers and toilets were on the lower level at the end of the building.

Upon arriving at our barracks, Sgt Haugen asked each of us into his office for a five-minute private meeting to get acquainted. All the rest were to wait their turn to be called. We were called in according to where our last names fell in the alphabet. Neperud, before O'Neil. It was finally my turn, and as my friend Nep comes out of the office there is a slight smirk on his face and the quick whisper to mention the name of Harry Haugen, who was a friend of ours from Eau Claire.

My turn. Sgt. Haugen says "welcome," followed by "Where are you from O'Neil?" to which I answer, "Eau Claire, Wisconsin, sir." He responded with the question "Do you know who I am?" To which I respond, "Yes sir, I believe you are Harry Haugen's Brother," to which he says, "Damn, you're right!" slaps his thigh and laughs at the coincidence of it all.

"Well," Sgt Haugen continues, "we're together for the next 11 weeks, and nobody needs to know we are from the same hometown. I will not let you guys get away with any mistakes. I will hold you to a higher standard so no one will be able to say you two had received more favorable treatment than others". So, here we were in the US Air Force in Texas, 1500 miles from home, and in our first hour, we had run into somebody from home. What a small world it must be.

On day one we went first for hair-cuts. The barbers took great pride in skinning those with "Duck Cuts", those of us who had arrived with crew cuts or close-cropped cuts received a cut to within ¼ inch of the scalp, short but not shaved. Most of us were between 18-21 years old and came from all over the eastern states ranging from Wisconsin, Minnesota, New York and New Hampshire to North Carolina, Alabama, Georgia, Florida and Texas. After hair-cuts, we marched to the dispensary for shots and medical checks. We all stood in line in our Skivvies to get shots. Several of the biggest of our group were shown to be big babies when the technicians came at them from both sides to inject using two needles simultaneously. Four shots in 5 seconds. The technicians took great personal pleasure in their work.

Then off to the tailor shop where we were quickly measured for boots, sox, underwear, one-piece (olive drab) fatigues (called coveralls in Eau Claire), dress blues, shirts, hats and caps. Like the barber shop and dispensary, the tailor shop was a machine, an efficient, no-nonsense high-performance production line. This was the U.S. Air Force.

During 11 weeks of Basic Training, we would learn about military discipline, and clear crisp salutes, about marching in perfect rhythm, skills in being neat & clean, living in close quarters, preparing for frequent inspections in housekeeping, marching and drilling, and the role of the United States Air Force in a world of uncertainties. Yes, and how to properly and efficiently clean pots and pans when working on KP. KP is not disciplinary, it is assigned to everyone in equal amounts, because we all eat in the mess-hall and everyone must do their share to help the cooks do their job.

Sgt Haugen was true to his word. He made sure we knew he was watching. A few weeks into learning the ropes, including marching, he appointed four of us, who seemed to "get the hang of it and appointed us "Squad Leaders," to lead 15 of our colleagues in all marching drills.

Sgt Haugen, Nep and I kept it a secret for eleven weeks. He announced it on our final day of basic training and true to his word he cut us no slack. He did however make me a squad leader about half way through Basic Training, I was proud of that.

In July 1954, we all left Basic Training with one stripe and on to our next base. Nep had qualified for Air Cadet training to fly, so he went to Waco Texas to await assignment. I went to Chanute Field, Illinois, south of Chicago, for an 11-month Aircraft Electrical Maintenance School. Rex Bolick a friend from Basic Training from Conover, North Carolina, was also assigned to the same school, and he ended up in the same barracks. Chanute AFB was a huge training base with many schools for aircraft mechanics, hydraulics, jet engines, reciprocating engines, helicopters, bombers and fighter aircraft instruments and even parachute packing.

Bolick and I had gotten along well during three months of Basic training. He called me a Yankee, and I called him a Hillbilly. He was the son of the postmaster in Conover, North Carolina and a smart, easy going, good old boy with a big heart. We often talked of home and our friends. I told him about Sandy and he talked of Shirley.

Sandy and I corresponded infrequently. She had graduated

63

from High School in June with Honors and began her nursing education at Abbott Hospital in Minneapolis, Minnesota, almost immediately. She was enrolled in a nursing program, which was three years, 36 straight months of training with lots of on-floor nursing experience, as well as specialized off-campus training at Minneapolis General Hospital and Mayo Clinic Rochester. All her academics in Anatomy, Physiology, Pharmacy, English and other fields were completed at Macalester College in St Paul.

Chanute AFB was located about 250 miles south of Chicago and another 250 miles to Eau Claire. The training in aircraft electrical systems was an eleven-month course continuing through mid-year 1955. And then we were to be assigned somewhere in the world where the USA had an airbase. The most dreaded possible places to end up were Thule Greenland and a spot in North Africa. It did occur to me that it would be very difficult to carry on a romance if I were stuck in Greenland or Africa.

Sandy and I were corresponding, and she would speak of going home for a weekend. I was determined to get home to see her. Public transportation was out of the question. Then, I recalled during the war young guys in military uniform would hitchhike. Drivers would favor them with rides because of the uniform. My duty hours ended at 16:00 hours (4PM) on Friday and began again at 08:00 hours (8AM) Monday. In that window of 60 hours, I decided I could hitch-hike to Eau Claire, enjoy seeing Sandy for an evening, see some other friends, my folks, and then hitchhike back to the base in Illinois within the window.

Having calculated it could be done, I decided to leave the Air Base on a Friday night and hitchhike home to Eau Claire, 500 miles ... And I did it ... multiple times... and several times with my friend Bolick, who Sandy would line up with a date. We were always back at the base Sunday evening. Had we not arrived back at the base by class time on Monday morning, we were considered AWOL. A risk we accepted.

In December 1954, all students were granted a ten-day Christmas Holiday leave. A fellow from the base was driving to Chicago and would give several of us a ride to the train station for $7. I bought a ticket to Eau Claire at the station and jumped on the train.

Unfortunately, Sandy was not going to be at home for Christmas. She was in her first year of her nursing school and, as an under-classman, she was assigned to work Christmas day on the floor at Abbott Hospital. She could not come home for Christmas Eve and she was heartbroken.

Since I was a little boy, Christmas Eve for our family was held at Grandpa Boiler's house in Baldwin, Wisconsin located midway between Eau Claire and Minneapolis. All the aunts, uncles, and cousins, nearly all living in Baldwin, would come there and be together for dinner and a big gift exchange.

The evening wore on and Uncle Don Bolier inquired about Sandy. He knew Sandy from the several times he had brought his car over to Eau Claire for us to drive to the prom. I told him she was in the dorm at Abbott because she had nurse duty the next morning. He handed me the keys and said, "Go see her." (My parents still did not own a family car and the company car was off-limits to me unless my Dad was in the car.)

The dorm was located near Abbott Hospital and close to downtown Minneapolis. It was Christmas Eve about 10 PM. I rang the doorbell, and the house-mother answered the bell. "I am here to see Sandra Tietge." When she came to the door, it was obvious she had been shedding some tears and was quite happy to

65

see me. We went to midnight Christmas Eve service at Westminster Presbyterian church in downtown Minneapolis then back to the dorm. I drove back to Baldwin.

I believe that was a turning point – from a somewhat casual dating relationship to a more serious romance for us. In reliving the experience, I brag about riding into Minneapolis on a white horse and sweeping her out of the grasp of Mother Abbott Hospital. In reality, I drove into Minneapolis in a white Oldsmobile and accompanied her to Christmas Eve candlelight service in the big and the stately Westminster Presbyterian Church. THANKS TO MY DEAR UNCLE DON!

(Note: Sixty-three years later on Christmas Eve 2017, Sandy and I attended the Christmas Eve service at Westminster for the first time since 1954. Mike, Susanne, Steve, Chris, Madeline and Rebecca all joined us for this memorable moment.)

I completed the course in Aircraft Electrical Systems in mid-1955 and received orders to report to Truax Field, Madison, Wisconsin for my first Permanent Party assignment. Quite the surprise! My classmates received assignments at U.S. Air-Force installations all over the world. I went to Madison, and my friend, Bolick, was assigned to the South Pacific Islands. I reported to Truax Field and spent the entire remainder of my enlistment there.

Madison is a clean, nice city in South Central Wisconsin nestled between two pretty lakes. It is home to the State Capitol, the University of Wisconsin, Truax Air Force Base, Ray-O-Vac and Oscar Meyer Wieners. During the war years of 1942-45, Truax had been a training base with thousands of GI's stationed there for months of radio operator training. During the weekends they were scattered throughout the community doing typical "guy stuff."

After the war ended in 1945 the base was closed, and the City Fathers and the fathers and mothers of daughters throughout the city breathed a sigh of relief. In about 1950, war broke out in Korea and the Cold War began to heat up. It was announced in Washington that Truax AFB was to be reactivated to accommodate an important component of the mission of the United States Air Defense Command. Its mission was to defend the United States from air attack from the North in the event the "Cold War" turned hot!

Madison was not happy with the base reopening. To soften the concerns, the newly assigned Base Commander arrived in Madison long before any troops came. He made contact with every Radio/TV station in the area, men's and women's service clubs, the Chamber of Commerce, church, school and civic groups to deliver the message. Truax AFB was required to be reopened to guard the northern tier of mid-west states in the event the USSR chose to advance their Cold War plan. Madison, Duluth, Minnesota, and two more bases in Michigan and North Dakota were established to deter any aircraft attempting to come in over the USA from the North.

The Truax AFB of the 1950's would have less than 3,000 troops, including professionally trained pilots and highly-trained mechanics and support staff, many married with young families. The base would be equipped with two squadrons of high-technology F-86D fighter aircraft. The new Base Commander was persuasive, and later, Madison offered warm greetings to the new troops and technicians with many thanks for the understanding shown by the US Air Force.

Truax AFB again began to hum. Construction of facilities for troops, lots of airplane hangars and a very sophisticated North American aircraft tracking facility were constructed. And then the airplanes came. The US Air Force did not call it an air show, but pilots flying in formations of four aircraft each began to reach Truax in close formation to cheers!

In the 50's, it was customary for all military personnel to be paid their monthly salary in cash. With more than 2,000 employees on base, the Commander decided to pay the entire base staff in $2.00 bills to demonstrate the economic power the base had in the area. The GI's paid their rent, gas, utilities, auto maintenance, groceries, medical bills, bar tabs and movie tickets in $2.00 bills. The huge economic force of the base was now well understood throughout "Badger land".

There were roughly 50 of these fighter-interceptor planes at this base, about six fully armed and in the air in minutes, and more could be airborne quickly. Duluth AFB, and the Michigan and North Dakota bases had firepower about equal so, theoretically, there were 200 of the latest, most modern, Air Force fighter jets in the world ready to defend the mid USA, if necessary. Gives one comfort.

In 1956, the Air Force replaced all of our airplanes with the newest, fastest, most technology-loaded fighter jet in the world. A machine with Delta wings, called the Delta-Dart, the F-102. This plane was loaded with more fire-power, speed, and maneuverability.

When the first four of these new planes were arriving at Truax we all scrambled out to the flight-line to watch. It was chilling to see these planes come in perfect diamond formation with delta wings forming the outer geometry like an arrow-head in fast flight.

My job was an 8-to-5 job subject to infrequent demands for the weekends. The job was not fulfilling. I was obligated to serve the

U.S. Air Force for eight years, four on active duty and four as a reserve (just in case the country got into more trouble). My enlistment began March 31, 1954, so I was obligated until March 1958, then the Reserves, preferably the inactive Reserves, until March 1962. I began to think about a life after the Air Force. I dearly loved being around aircraft, and the business of defending our country from aggressive outside forces was a charge to "Patriotic Loyalty" for me. I just did not see myself in uniform forever.

I would go up before a Board of Review for consideration to be promoted with another stripe. When asked about my long-term interests, I could with confidence answer that "I expect to complete my enlistment obligation and then become a civilian with a college degree and a family." The plan unfolding in my head was to bone up on my high-school math skills, prepare for a college experience through aid of the GI-Bill, find my way in the world of business and marry Sandra Tietge!

I was 21 years old, and I think I've finally got my shit together now!

And, as components of my new personal plan I enrolled in an algebra course in an evening class to spruce up my math skills. And, for nearly two years I maintained a part-time evening/weekend job in a theater in Madison accumulating cash for a ring and for school. My Air-Force short list days 'til-discharge was on the wall.

If Sandy and I were to plan a wedding it was important I obtain the approval of her family. I had never been so nervous as on the evening I asked for her parents Harold and Cozy Tietge approval to marry their daughter. Her dad Harold, an executive and plant Manager for the big Dolly Madison Milk and Ice Cream plants in Eau Claire, was a gentle soft spoken, U of Iowa Graduate in Dairy Technology. He had an intuition for mechanical equipment and people. Her Mom, Cozette, Cozy for short, was a daughter of a small-town pharmacist in West Central Iowa. She had been educated, like my mother, to teach, however during the Great Depression jobs were very scarce. Cozy was the epitome of a homemaker.

Sandy's family included herself, the oldest at age 20, Mike, five years younger, Dennis, nine years younger and Cheryl, thirteen years younger. Mike and I would go out to the driveway for a game of horse on the basketball court. He was a fine athlete and frequently beat me at my game.

The parents approved my request to marry their daughter. It was then I discovered I also had to obtain the ok from Cozy's two brothers, a very "niece" protective pair of well educated, hard drinking, card savvy, raw story telling characters out of the 1930's. These two were a pair of honest and fiercely loyal family brothers. Arthur Miller, a graduate of a U of California medical school in 1939, Charles Miller, educated at the master's level in the early 1940's at Kansas State having been disqualified for military service by an injury. The two would do their best to test me.

They felt it was necessary to test my confidence for marrying their niece and ... I passed!

WEDDING BELLS IN THE DISTANCE

Sandy and I were writing more often, we were scheduling weekends in Eau Claire to be together, and we were beginning to talk of a wedding. She was in nurse's training until September 1957, I was enlisted in the Air Force until March of 1958.

In May 1956, I attended a dinner/dance the student nurses organized in Minneapolis. It was a very nice party and midway through, while we were alone and the others were dancing, I brought out the ring. She was pleased, I was pleased, and when the others returned to the table after the music stopped, they noticed and they were pleased. Two of them were in our wedding later.

In late 1956, the Korean war had been over for several years, and the US Government decided to order a reduction of forces in the military. My friend, Bob Neperud, who was handling all the orders to come down to a small Air Force Base in Southern Minnesota, called excitedly because an order had just come through from HQ that military personnel with normal discharge dates between January and June of 1958 (that was us) could receive their honorable discharge up to six months early provided they had been accepted by a college or university. Bingo!

While searching for a future path in the past few years, I had decided on a Business Administration Major and a Psychology minor believing that the study of human behavior would be useful in dealing with customers, employees and service providers in the business world. Nep had decided to pursue a teaching degree and majored in the sciences. We both applied to University of Wisconsin at Eau Claire and were accepted for the spring semester beginning January, 1958.

Sandy was through with her training in September 1957, I was going to be discharged in November 1957… Let's plan a wedding! The date of December 28, 1957, was chosen. The church would be fully decorated for Christmas, Sandy would join the staff at Luther Hospital in Eau Claire and my college career would begin in January.

November 1, 1957 was the day of my discharge from the US Air Force. It was five months early and I was accepted at the College of my choice, and I was about to be married to the love of my life! Was this a great day or what?

The wedding plans were well under way and did not need much of my contributions. I was out of the military and needed a job for a few weeks. I could start right after Wisconsin Deer Hunting. In the 1950's, the U.S. Post office delivered mail to home routes twice daily during the Christmas card mail season. I signed on as Seasonal Mail Carrier and delivered mail on a walking route for three weeks in December 1957.

In the 1950's, many of the downtown buildings and many homes on the south side of downtown were reflecting Victorian styling. The Lumber Barons had lots of money and wanted to show it in their homes, offices and churches. Eau Claire's First Presbyterian Church was classic. It was constructed in the late 1800's when Eau Claire was a hot town with a logging industry including saw-mills and many assorted industry support companies as a basis for its commercial wealth. Many City Fathers owed their wealth to the native White Pine forests of Northern Wisconsin. The church exterior, as well as the sanctuary, were classically designed reflecting Victorian styling.

This was the church where Sandy and I had met six years earlier on a Sunday evening in 1951. The church was beautifully decked out for a Christmas wedding with loads of red and green foliage. Our Pastor, Charles Melcher, was a very proper Pennsylvanian with a Divinity Degree from Princeton University.

Our wedding was complete with attendants - including Sandy's nursing school buddies, Joyce Kietzman and Mary Sorenson. I had Best Man, George Losby, a sincere friend since

Boy Scout days, and Bob Neperud, my Air Force colleague. Dennis, Sandy's younger brother, and my cousin Neil Norelius and several friends acted as ushers and groomsmen. Cheryl, Sandy's little sis, was our flower girl. And our parents and families were happy.

Note: George Losby and I were 15 when we made the pact to be each other's best man. We had been in Scouting together, fishing friends, double dated many times with he and Sharon Kelly. We were on the same route to school and walked to school together nearly every day for three years. George and Sharon were married several months before Sandy and I and were living in an apartment on State Street in Eau Claire.

Sandy and I honeymooned in Chicago. We left Eau Claire with $112 cash, a two-day reservation at the LaSalle Hotel, a classic old hotel in the Chicago Loop at $12 per day, and hearts full of togetherness.

We did museums, marveled at the loop, the elevated trains overhead, the big stores and endless traffic. The New York Company doing My Fair Lady was in town. I asked the Concierge if tickets might be available. He answered yes ... at $22 each. Enough, that we opted for a 3D movie as an alternative. I think it may have been featuring "Around the World In 80 Days".

The weather was getting nasty, snow was on the way and with temps about 30, it promised to be sloppy. The third Day, New Year's Eve day 1957, we checked out and headed back to Eau Claire... in near blizzard conditions.

Don and Sharon Severson were good friends, had attended our wedding and advised us to stop in Madison on our return trip from Chicago. Don was in the University of Wisconsin Med School, and they had a small apartment near the campus. We arrived in Madison late in the day after nearly eight hours on the snowy two-lane highway (US 12).

We found a motel near Middleton, registered for the night and called. Sharon was thrilled, ("We knew you were coming!") and they drove on out to meet us at our motel. My best man, George Losby, had given us a bottle of Champagne for a wedding gift. The Severson's and the O'Neil newlyweds consumed the bottle and walked across the highway to a nightclub where we spent New Year's Eve 1957.

We celebrated New Year's Eve with the Seversons for the next 59 consecutive years!

<u>1958: A New Beginning</u>
<u>MARRIED COLLEGE STUDENTS</u>

Our first little one-bedroom apartment was in an old house on Marston Ct. in Eau Claire at $50 per month, sharing a bath with a geezer in the adjacent apartment, but otherwise cozy. We accumulated some surplus furniture from our parents, bought a sofa, and a used 1930's vintage refrigerator. My folks gave us a television for a wedding present, Sandy's folks kicked in a roll-a-way for our overnight guests, a library table and other things. Sandy's brother Mike and his girlfriend placed a decorated Christmas tree in our apartment while we were on our honeymoon. We built a bookcase from boards and bricks, added a couple of lamps and a table and chairs and we were good to go.

After years of agonizing over my career plan, or lack thereof, I was enrolled to study for the degree in Business Administration with a minor in Psychology. Because of my Military education in aircraft electrical systems, I was awarded 8 science credits by the University of Wisconsin, Eau Claire, a great help in qualifying for the BS with my Bachelor's Degree.

Sandy landed a great job in OB as delivery room nurse at Luther Hospital in Eau Claire, so she was at work in her career. I was paid $110 per month under the GI Bill. Paid my first semester fees of $88 tuition and $12 book rent. Our parents had us over for dinner often, we drove an old 1954 Dodge sedan which was paid for with Air Force earnings.

My first semester began in January,1958. I did not work the first semester, needing to fully concentrate on my studies because of my under-developed high school study habits. The first day at college was a wake-up call. Though many of the students on campus were vets like me, many more were fresh faces just out of high school, some 17 others 18 years old. I was 23, married and just out of the military. I was nearly a geezer in this place. My study skills were rusty, my English Composition skills were a disaster. English 101 was my first big challenge. I received a big red "F" on my first 13 papers. Fortunately, I put together a good term-paper which salvaged a "C" for the course for me.

Then, one fine day in about 1958, I discovered my old friend Billy Bonesho on Campus. We ran into each other near the mailboxes on campus. I had seen Bill only twice since his family relocated to Spring Brook, Wisconsin in the early 1940's. Once when I was in his area on a fishing trip with my friend "Ade" and once in the Fall of 1952 when he was attending Eau Claire as a recent graduate of Spooner High and playing quarterback for the college team. We spoke for about three minutes through the fence. But, now it's 1958, we're both married, veterans of military service and in college. Quite a coincidence. We got our wives to meet each other and they hit it off. Both were putting their husbands through college and as kindred spirits, we began to get together often.

Bill and I rediscovered how our family histories had merged ... again. The Bonesho's and the O'Neil families were connected back to the early 1900's in St Croix Falls. Bill's grandfather and mine were acquainted, and our dads were high school classmates at St. Croix Falls High School in the 1920's as were our dad's sisters, two each. When our little family moved to Eau Claire in the late 1930's, the Mott and Mary Bonesho family did the same. In 1940, at age 5, Billy and I became friends in Eau Claire.

Unfortunately, in about 1943, the Bonesho family relocated to Spring Brook, Wisconsin, near Spooner. The friendship went dormant until Bill and I reconnected at the university mail-boxes in 1958 and, to this day, we remain very close friends.

While I struggled with studies, I discovered I am not alone. Most of our college friends were in the same condition, married, military veterans, no kids. Bob Neperud, Air Force, earning a teaching degree; George Losby, Army, pre-law student and would transfer to the University of Wisconsin after two years; Tom Hanson, Navy, earning a teaching degree; and Bill Bonesho, Navy, working on a teaching degree.

After my first semester in June, 1958, I needed a summer job. Dick and Jim Gillett, co-owners of Eau Claire Food Lockers, hired me to drive their truck and deliver frozen vegetables, seafood, and fruit to local grocery stores.

Sandy and I had discussed having children and were in agreement that three possibly four, would be the right number. We surmised we would have them while we're young so we could grow up with them and enjoy some activities together such as travel, camping and playing basketball in the driveway.

In early 1958, Sandy developed a pain in her abdomen. It did not take the Dr. long to diagnose a tubal pregnancy, and she was in surgery quickly. Her mother, Cozy, was extremely concerned, because her (Cozy's) mother had died from a tubal pregnancy. We had concerns that since one tube was now gone, she may have trouble getting pregnant. However, she had no trouble and had three successful pregnancies.

Labor Day weekend 1958, friends George Losby (Ade) and Sharon suggested we two couples go on a camping trip to Canada. He and Sharon had some gear, Sandy and I scrounged gear from friends. The Saturday morning of departure was overcast and somewhat threatening. We had carefully loaded up Georges Jeep Wagon with tents, warm clothes, rain gear, sleeping bags, air mattresses, great breakfast and dinner fixens, a case of beer and even a picnic table canvas in case we needed cover while we were eating.

We drove up Minnesota Highway 61, crossed into Canada and drove west of Thunder Bay, Ontario, to beautiful Kakabeka Falls Provincial Park ... all in the rain. The rain stopped long enough for us to erect our tents, tie the tarp over the picnic table, drink a beer and prepare supper. It was turning colder, and the rain began again. We decided to turn in about 10 PM. I went out from the covered picnic table to prepare the tent Sandy and I would share that night. The air mattresses were floating in an inch of water, sleeping bags were in danger of getting wet and here comes Sandy from the under the cover of the picnic table.

Sandy was a novice camper and already somewhat skeptical about this entire event. She put one knee inside the tent and said something nasty to me. Sandy and Sharon slept in the car, "Ade" and I slept in his tent, a bit dryer than mine. In the morning, we woke to an inch of fresh snow and the temperature at 30 degrees. We packed up and bailed out. I thought sure this would be the shortest marriage on record, but the second night as we were heading home, we found a nice motel on Minnesota's North Shore. The hot shower was terrific.

Sandy fortunately had an appropriate memory loss, and on the following Labor Day, George and Sharon, Tom and Mary Jo Hanson and Sandy and I piled into the Jeep with all our gear and headed for more camping fun at Wisconsin's Copper Falls and Pattison State parks. Weather was great, camping was enjoyable and memorable.

AND THEN THERE WERE THREE - AND THEN THERE WERE FOUR

The first semesters in college were very challenging and I wound up on probation with a GPA of less than 2.0. I was working quite a few hours per week at Johnson Motors on Water Street. School was challenging, but one day in May of 1959, Michael Eugene O'Neil, showed up. What a thrill for us, and the grand-parents were nuts. Everyone wanted to hold him, smooch him and care for him.

We had moved to a different apartment in town, a bit more spacious but on the second floor of an old house on Hudson Street. It was a very hot summer. The second floor was so hot I would go outside and spray cold water from the outside faucet onto the hot roof and second story walls to try and cool off the house. We three would go for rides in the car with the windows open to get a hint of air movement to cool us.

The best part of this situation were the landlords, Cecil and Mary Johnson, who were very nice people in their 40's. Cecil and his brother owned Johnson Motors, a farm/auto supply retail store on Water street and they hired me to work the city desk and sell goods over the counter. I worked 50 hours per week to make $50 per week. I sold auto parts and plow-shares, overalls and denim jackets. In the fall I was back at school but worked every evening and Saturday ... at a buck an hour.

My Father-in-law, Harold Tietge, discovered I work 50 hours a week at one dollar per hour, and he vowed to improve that situation. Harold was the Plant Manager at Dolly Madison Dairies and he steers the foreman to interview me for a summer dairy plant job. I started in the summer beginning at $1.87 per hour, filling in for vacationing employees. My job is at the end of the filling machine where half pints, pints, quarts and half gallons come off the filler at a torrid rate. I must have done well, because I received a couple of raises.

Then it was back to school for Fall semester. There was an opening on the afternoon shift loading trucks, just a perfect fit for managing class schedules and other duties as husband and Dad.

Friend and Air Force colleague, Bob Neperud, (Nep) had worked at Dolly Madison prior to our Air Force enlistment and was back working at the Dairy as we both launched into our college work as married veterans. Nep knew the dairy well, having been there for more than a year before our Air Force enlistment. When he got his hands on the controls of the filling machine and I was on the take-a-way end, he would crank up the filler to high speed in an attempt to bury me! He failed.

My friend Bill Bonesho, (Bones) also needed a job and applied at Dolly Madison. His Navy experience was three years on a

79

submarine where every crew-member must learn and understand every single pipe and valve on the entire boat. He was hired and worked evenings, a perfect fit with his class schedule. He reported in after the day crew has completed all its bottling, and each and every tank, valve and pipe must be cleaned and sanitized for the next day's bottling run. Bill had the perfect background for the job.

Sandy was working nights, I was in school and working evenings. Cozy was our go-to lady for Mike. She and Mike developed a special kind of relationship. My folks would take Mike some of the time, but it was generally Cozy. It was Mike who named her forever "Nonnie".

By 1961, we had another baby on the way and due in August. Sandy got out to shop for a new apartment because now we needed a bit more space for two youngsters. She found and rented the lower level of a remodeled duplex on Doty Street on Eau Claire's East side, having a large laundry room, which doubles as a nursery.

Our friends, George and Sharon Losby, rented the upper level unit of this duplex. They had no children but had a small dog to enjoy. George and I were originally friends through Boy Scouting, then through High School. Sandy and I double dated with George and Sharon many times through the years and had a strong relationship to the extent George and I made a pact to be each other's best man when the time came. They were married on March 9 1957, and we were married December 28, 1957. We were each other's "Best Man".

Regularly we would need a bit of extra help in making class schedules merge properly with Mike's naps and meal schedule. For some time, Sandy worked nights in the delivery room. We would feed Mike in the morning then Sandy would go to bed and

I would drop Mike off at Nonnie's for the day en-route to my class at school. Later in the day, we would pick Mike up a grandma's house and take him home, then go to work at the dairy.

Occasionally, we needed more creativity. George would have early classes and early out, my first class would begin at 1PM. So, Mike would go to school with me, George finishes his class at 12:50, we meet in the parking lot, transfer Mike to George's car and he takes him home and puts him down for his nap.

Our good friends, the Losby's, were going on to law School at the University of Wisconsin, Madison, in 1960. The upstairs apartment was open, and Bill and Carole Bonesho were looking for new digs. They had a new baby on the way and with Bill now working at Dolly Madison and a very convenient location, they moved into our upstairs.

Many of our married friends were students. The house we rented became the frequent venue for party time with married vets in college, some with children. Carole and Bill Bonesho, who had lived in San Diego for a time following his discharge from the Navy treated us all our party goers to a new taste sensation ... the taco. There were no taco shops in Eau Claire in 1959 and this was a terrific taste. We said, "we should start a taco shop in Eau Claire. Within a few years Taco John, Taco Bell and others were popping up everywhere.

After the birth of Mary Jo Bonesho, the two moms, Sandy and Carole, really bonded while pushing their babies in strollers through the cemetery close by our Doty Street apartments. As students, we clung together because we were all poor, working part-time, a few with children, and just trying to claw our way through school and finally get a real job and a real career.

STEVE ARRIVES

In August 1961, little Steven Leslie O'Neil is born. A live wire from the time he left the womb. Mom and Dad were very proud as are all in the family. Having these two sons and working at the hospital, Sandy was a trooper. The entire family pitched in to help with baby sitting and giving her breaks.

When Steve arrived, I was entering my last semester, a Fall semester at the newly named University of Wisconsin, Eau Claire. I was able to graduate in four years with a 32-credit Bachelor of Science Degree in Business Administration and a 23-credit minor in Psychology ... and a 2.0 GPA benefitting from an "A" in a semester finale course in Speech and Oral Presentation.

Chapter 5
CORPORATE AMERICA: THE GREATEST UNIVERSITY

GRADUATION AND A "REAL JOB"

The final months of 1961 were even busier than normal. Classes to wrap up the graduation credits and launching a job search campaign were each demanding. My school, extremely well regarded and with a long track record back to 1916 in training teachers, was not well known as an institution of Business Administration Graduates. In fact, I was in the original class to graduate with a Bachelor's in Business Administration Degree from The University of Wisconsin, Eau Claire.

Since job opportunities in Eau Claire for new Business Graduates were limited, Sandy and I had chosen to job-search in the Twin Cities of Minneapolis St Paul and Southern Wisconsin to remain near our families and roots. My credentials and resume were limited to part-time jobs while a student, 3 ½ years in the U.S. Air Force with hands-on aircraft experience and my college course work in Business and Psychology.

I began interviewing for work as a new college grad by visiting Employers Mutual of Wausau. Warner Brake and Clutch in

Beloit, Wisconsin, extended an offer to join their HR Department and Birds Eye Foods in Waseca MN offered a similar position. Proctor and Gamble offered a position of servicing P&G goods in shelves in grocery stores. So far nothing lit up the board for me.

1962-66: THE HONEYWELL DAYS

Honeywell Aero Division extended an offer to join their organization in a position in manufacturing and production scheduling. Everyone knew of Honeywell as Minneapolis Honeywell, one of the top US manufacturers of controls for residential and commercial HVAC applications. They were lesser known to the public, but well established in the aircraft fuel control and guidance systems business. The Aerospace business was coming on very strong as the USA discovered Russia was ahead in the cold war race. Bingo! I like this. And my love affair with aircraft, which began by making models of WW II airplanes back in the 1940's could be furthered by this job.

My job as a Production Control Coordinator began in early February 1962 and we were happy guys at our house. I was thrilled with the opportunity and dug in with great vigor to learn the business. We produced products for many types of military and civilian aircraft. Customers were the aircraft manufacturers, major US and foreign air-lines and the US Government purchasing for the military versions.

I discovered an entire company of Honeywell Aero Division in Northeast Minneapolis, which became my introduction to an understanding of modern industry. Little did I know that two years later I would be very involved with the production and delivery of state-of-the-art equipment to NASA which would place American Astronauts on the surface of the Moon in 1969.

During my Air Force career, I worked evenings and weekends off-base for two years at a Madison theater to supplement my very modest military earnings of $144 per month. "To stash cash for a ring and for school" was my plan. Now in 1962, I have my wife, two sons, a degree and a great new job. I began the search for housing in the N/E Minneapolis area. We needed a two-bedroom apartment in a clean and safe area near my work at Honeywell. I found nothing to suit my family needs and became more determined and creative.

Sandy's Uncle Charles Miller, her mom's bro, to the rescue. He contacted a friend, Keith Nelson, in the St Paul Real Estate business. Within days, Keith Nelson and Uncle Charles had identified a three-year-old, three-bedroom Rambler in Roseville (a good young suburb with good schools) for sale at a reasonable price of $15,500. The house had a good kitchen, unfinished basement, 2-car garage, extra deep lot and an assumable VA mortgage at a reasonable rate of 4¼% interest.

It had not occurred to us to consider buying a house at this time, but between Keith Nelson's generosity in reducing his commission a bit as a token of friendship with Uncle Charles, a little something extra from Uncle Charles, a contribution from my parents and the $500 in savings bond's I had stashed away during my Air Force time "for a ring or school "... we bought the house! It was a perfect size at 960 Sq. Ft, terrific location, nice kids in the neighborhood, big yard, safe street, easy drive to work at Honeywell and close to a good school.

We could not close until April 1, and my job began February 11. Again, Uncle Charles and Mary Ellen Miller (the same Mary Ellen who had suggested to niece Sandra she should go to the Sunday evening Senior High fellowship meeting to meet some kids in January 1952) came to the rescue. I moved in with

Charles, Maryellen and their two daughters, Carol and Nancy, for the seven weeks until our own house was ready. I would go home to Eau Claire every Friday and return on Sunday evening.

After closing on April 1, 1962, we began a very intensive cleaning, repairing and repainting project with lots of family help. Sandy's folks, my folks, Charles and Mary Ellen and Uncle Red Norwick all pitched in to help. Within a few days we were ready to move in to 2744 Virginia Ave in Roseville, Minnesota. It would serve us well for the next eight years.

We located a new Church, The Presbyterian Church of the Way, on Lexington Ave and found it to be full of families very much like ours. It was founded in 1959, and the new church building was completed in 1961. We began to make friends quickly and our young sons made friends. Sandy and I were soon the Senior High Fellowship group advisors, we taught Sunday School, and served as Deacon, Elder, and members of various committees. The Jack and Eadie Allison family and the Ted and Teddy Bergstrom family became especially close. In fact, the Allison, Bergstrom and O'Neil boys began a series of father/son hunting, fishing, camping ventures, which went on for over 30 consecutive years.

Honeywell is an old Minneapolis company, best known for heating and air conditioning controls. The Aero Division was a lesser-known branch of this company. In the 1960's, the Aero Division was a major player in manufacturing fuel measurement and guidance controls systems for the aircraft of the world. Boeing, McDonnell Douglas, Grumman, North American Aviation and many others, including the military and civilian versions of those company's aircraft, were customers of Honeywell.

Upon my hiring in February 1962 I was assigned to a department and spent several weeks shadowing Dick Larson, an experienced man. As I became more experienced, I worked with less supervision and took over a desk responsible for a number of bread and butter products. Ted Kondrak was my coach and guide through this next level. As time wore on and I seemed to be getting the hang of it, several newer less seasoned products were added to my portfolio. Soon I had been there a year, working hard and getting a raise was a good experience.

My original supervisor was Jim Murphy, a St. Paul Irishman with a ready smile and a savvy mind. Later Jim was promoted to supervise the Contracts Administration Department and was replaced by Dick Converse, a former US Marine during the Korean affair. Dick had a tough outer skin but he drove himself every bit as hard as any of us who worked for him. Dick and I were to remain friends for 40 years.

In 1964 on May 12, a third son, David Charles, arrived. We had a bedroom for him and two older brothers to teach him the ropes of the neighborhood. Dave was a Midway Hospital, St Paul baby. He was nearly a Snelling Avenue baby. It was the middle of the night when Dave said "I want out." I was driving as fast as I dared, almost hopeful a policeman would notice my speeding and escort me to the hospital. We arrived at Midway, Sandy went into the ER, and I looked for a parking spot. By the time I had parked the car and got back in the hospital, Dave was here. Welcome Dave, we're your family!

Back at the factory, Dick Converse my supervisor, and I had a meeting at which time he spoke of a higher position available to me, which he called "New Development." In this position, I would be responsible for some exotic new fuel measurement products for the Saturn Booster, the big NASA brute of the new space age, just in development and on an extreme schedule to design, develop, test and produce in small quantities.

At the moment I was not clear of the mission, but it soon became apparent this was a big deal. It was 1964 and President Kennedy had announced, "We will put a man on the moon by 1969!" My new products were the heart of the fuel measurement and fuel consumption system of the Saturn Booster, the biggest and 'baddest' rocket for space exploration in all of the world at the time. An example of the Saturn Booster may be seen today on the main floor at the National Space Center Museum in Florida.

I had a "Top-Secret" clearance while in the Air Force and again would be required to have a high security clearance. I had the power of Honeywell, The United States Government and NASA to secure, with priority, whatever materials and components were needed for this project on an expedited basis. And, because of the nature of the fuel mixture on the Saturn, only certain types of aluminum, stainless steel and other components were to be used. I was required to maintain precise records of the exact source where every piece of material used in construction had come from and obtain a certification of the chemical properties of each piece. The danger was that even a harmless screw placed in the Oxygen/Hydrogen environment could cause the entire system to explode on the pad or in the air.

My job was exciting and demanding. I was shepherd of that project for two years working very long hours. And in 1969, when the USA landed and Neil Armstrong and Buzz Aldrin walked on the moon, I busted a few buttons for my part. There were thousands of others who did lots more, but this was a big deal for a kid from the Eighth Ward in Eau Claire, Wisconsin.

In 1965, my former Production Control Supervisor, Jim Murphy, called me to talk. The Saturn project was doing well, I was not as challenged as in the days of early development and a bit restless for more challenge and more money. Jim offered me a position as a Contract Administrator, working with purchasing agents doing business with Honeywell. I accepted, and soon Boeing, McDonald-Douglas and Grumman Aircraft were the first customers I would inherit from another fellow.

I enrolled in the evening training led by Honeywell legal people in a class entitled "Government Contract Law." The course was tailored to the relationships with big league customers including aircraft manufacturers, airlines and the US Air Force. The course supplemented the Business Law I had studied at Eau Claire.

Unfortunately, the job turned out to be less than I expected. It was nobody's error, it just did not have the excitement I had hoped for. I was a candidate for change.

NEW CHALLENGES AND EXPERIENCES

A few months into my Honeywell job as Contract Administrator, I received a call from Bob Jonason, an ex-Honeywell fellow who was aware of my Production Control work and had just been named Manager of Manufacturing at a smaller firm in New Brighton, Minnesota. He needed someone to take over as Production Control Manager for Setchell-Carlson, a forty-year-old manufacturer of electronics products, including radio and television.

The company was producing high-quality, home color TV's in furniture-quality cabinets, and they had a run-a-way horse on their hands. After careful consideration I accepted the position and left Honeywell. The market for home color TV was explosive – so explosive, that Zenith, RCA and several other giants were entering the market with great products that had superior electronics and a well-established United States network of dealers. The new technology of solid-state electronics destroyed the Setchell-Carlson business in two years, ending the business and my job.

1967- 1976: GRACO DAYS

It was 1967, and I was on the job market after the failure of Setchell-Carlson. I Joined Graco, a $27MM (*Note: Over a $1.0 billion in 2018*) Minneapolis manufacturing company with a strong reputation for products and services in the pumping, metering, measuring and dispensing of fluid materials. Graco pumps were used world-wide in applications in automobile servicing, food handling, painting and decorating work ranging from spraying picket fences to bridges and ships and fine automobile finishes.

I was hired as Customer Service Manager by John Gray and his boss, Wally Salovich, the Marketing VP. This department worked closely with sales and a long list of distributors throughout the US, South America and Europe. I was responsible for management of Order Entry and Warehousing and Shipping, including export.

At one point, our system had developed a problem of order-bloat. Too many orders, which overwhelmed the manufacturing system, plugged up the channels and left customers waiting for parts. I volunteered to install a system I had used at Honeywell for expediting and streamlining product and parts orders in a manufacturing system. My supervisor gave me the authority, and

I formed a project to "break the backlog". Because I was being quite intense to get the job done, somebody named the project the "Irish Devil Project" with Gene as the "Devil Himself." Amused, I ordered green lapel badges and rubber stamps of the image of a leprechaun holding a devil's spear with three sharp forks. Every person assigned to the project wore the badge and carried the stamp with a pad of Kelly-green ink. We shipped over 5,000 backlogged orders in about 30 days. Everyone was pleased with the results, and we all got a few atta boys. Many years later and long after I had left Graco, I was at an event with several old Graco colleagues – one of whom told me he still had the Irish Devil Rubber Stamp among his memorabilia.

Within a few months, I was approached by the head of Manufacturing and was asked to take on the Materials Management Functions of Production Control, Purchasing and Distribution. I now had a team, was getting leadership experience and loving it. We made improvements in performance in all departments. buying with lower costs, scheduling with better results and shipping with higher on-time and accuracy performance.

In 1968, the O'Neil family had grown to five. Our third son David was four. The three boys were active in youth hockey and baseball. As a family, we did some camping, fishing and other get-a-ways like summer vacations at Burntside Lake near Ely Minnesota and weekends at the cabin in the woods of Polk County, Wisconsin. And, nearly always, the July 4th picnic at Aunt Hazel and Uncle Vic's cabin on Bear Trap Lake near Amery.

Our old cars gave up, and we finally bought a new Ford Station Wagon. This was a big deal to have a car with less than 50,000 miles when we bought it. It was a great vehicle. We had driving trips to North Carolina to see Sandy's brother's family, Mike, Terry, Mark and Jill. On a side trip we saw the sights of Washington DC. Later, Glacier Park, Jasper and Banff to see the beauty of the Rocky Mountains.

There was a new addition in the future for our family. The little girl we needed to complete our family was due to arrive in March of 1970. We decided we needed a larger house and located a custom home-builder to build it for us in Shoreview, a near suburb of St Paul. Sandy had developed a strong sense for home design, furnishing and décor. She was in her happy place planning and decorating the new house. We cemented the deal with the contractor and, because the property was full of Oak trees, the family became involved in lot tree clearance. Over Memorial Day weekend, my dad came over from Eau Claire with his chain saw and other tools, and we cleared the lot of 42 Oak trees. The boys were involved in dragging branches into large piles which would be burned later.

During construction, we visited the site nearly every day to inspect the work completed and marvel at the progress. Other homes were under construction at the time, and our new neighbors-to-be were also visiting the site. Gerry and Sandy Crest and Tony and Dottie Senarighi would inspect their new place as well.

In September 1969, we moved into a five-bedroom, two-story colonial home with a formal dining room, two fire-places, double garage and space galore, located on a beautiful wooded property. It was a wonderful experience for all of us and the big reward for visiting the site nearly every day during construction.

The USA landed a man on the moon in July 1969. Our carpenters were so excited, they wrote a note on the side of the house just before the siding went on noting, "Our boys landed on the moon today." My buttons were busting a bit too, the Saturn program I worked on so hard at Honeywell was a part of it all.

Back at Graco, Ken Hiebel and I got acquainted. We would lunch together often and followed it with a short walk around the neighborhood to get a bit of fresh air. Ken was a Minnesota native, married, two children and a degree from St Thomas University We shared a common interest, investing in real estate and spoke about building an investment portfolio in rental Real Estate.

In 1974, Ken, Joann, Sandy and I purchased a 15-unit apartment building through our Real Estate friend, Keith Nelson. This property, containing 1, 2 and 3-bedroom units, was located in St. Paul just east of I-35E near Maryland. The price was $150,000. We determined the property was under-market priced because it needed cosmetic improvements, most of which Ken and I and our talented wives, Joann and Sandy, were able to provide. The seller was offering a Contract for De

We scrounged up $7,500 each, agreed to the terms of the contract and assumed the first mortgage on the property. Now we were owners with several bad eggs in the nest and lots of cosmetic improvements to make. Nearly every weekend was a work weekend at the apartment building. As a unit emptied, we would fix it up with new flooring, complete paint job, wallpapering and other upgrades. The bad eggs received the most attention from us, up to and including a firm invitation to move out.

Within 18 months, all apartments were cleaned up, repaired, repainted, newly carpeted and new appliances where needed. We stripped the laundry room and repainted and placed new washers and dryers on new vinyl floors. We painted all the hallways and replaced the carpet. We raised the rents and placed a rigid rule for on-time payment of rents. We each retained our jobs, worked on the apartments nights and weekends as required, and a trickle of cash flow began.

INVESTMENT STRATEGIES

During the war years, my parents urged me to be thrifty and support the war effort. Dimes placed in war bonds would grow over ten years. Eighteen dollars would grow to twenty-five dollars in ten years. In my military years, I managed to save even a small amount from meager earnings, which ranged from $78 per month up to $144 per month at my discharge. I put the money in US Savings bonds, which grew to $500 by the time I needed the cash.

Since 1962, my first line of investment is always the home I live in. Later, In the 60's, I tried investing in the securities markets. I signed on for a class taught by a securities salesman for a Minneapolis Stock Brokerage firm. He taught the basics and referred the class members to several publications for informative reading.

When I finally felt a degree of comfort, I bought a small amount of low-priced stocks. A plastics manufacturer and a North Dakota Oil Company were on my first buy list. Unfortunately, I was not aware of the wisdom of Warren Buffet, who even today advises, "do not buy a stock if you do not intend to hold for at least ten years." I sold too soon, and discovered I was not a good stock picker because of these and other transactions.

I founded an Investment Club among neighbors and friends. We met at our home monthly. There may have been ten members at one time and we put in ten dollars per month. The careers of the members were varied, and I thought the wider and varied backgrounds could benefit the group. No, most just preferred a few of us study and select the stocks. They would continue throwing in their ten bucks depending on a few of us deciding on buy/sell strategy. This was not working well, and then we discovered with contributions coming in every month and an occasional sell or withdraw, we nearly had to have bookkeeping like a mutual fund. Too much bookwork broke up the club.

Then I attempted to learn the Commodities market. Sandy had a cousin in Iowa trading in pork bellies nearly every week and appeared to be doing well. A friend and I each contributed $500 to a brokerage account and we began to watch corn futures. When the time was right, we bought a contract of 5,000 bushels of corn for our thousand dollars and accepted an obligation to accept the corn by the following November or sell the contract at a profit sooner. It did not happen, and we lost our $500. I decided this was too fast for my conservative bones, so I told my partner I was withdrawing, grateful I only lost $500.

A few years later I began a long-term affair with mutual funds and, after real estate, they're the best form of securities investment for me. The funds I buy are from Fidelity Funds, no-load, professionally managed and professional stock picking. A management fee of well under 1% per year is assessed, and Fidelity Funds have been an excellent investment alternative for us over the past 30 years.

THE YOUNG O'NEIL FAMILY

It was our intent to have a little girl in our family. Sandy had given birth to the three boys and had experienced some problems with the third pregnancy, so we began the adoption process. In March of 1970, little Sara arrived. We had worked with Children's Home Society of St Paul attending counseling, passed all their tests and waited, and waited for nine months. When the day arrived that we were to go meet Sara, not yet 30 days old, the boys were ready and away we went. Everyone held Sara and when the time came, we bundled her up and headed for her new home and her new bedroom. Our parents and friends were happy for us. All the boys were anxious to take her for walks in the stroller and were very attentive to her needs.

With my interest in basketball I was hopeful our boys would play the game. But no, they all wanted hockey sticks, and for the next 15 years we were a hockey family. Hockey practice was held two evenings a week on outdoor ice, one or two games a week on outdoor ice. Dads removed the snow from the ice prior to game time. Every year, their feet would grow and larger skates were required. I began to buy hockey sticks a dozen at a time. We advanced to travel teams and then to weekend tournaments at places like Rochester and Duluth.

For one memorable period in the 1970's, we had two boys on travel teams and the other son on an in-house team. On Friday's, I would get home from work at 5:30, we would eat quickly and load up the Suburban with hockey gear and head for the first hockey event of 7 scheduled on the weekend. The truck never got cooled off with the last event of the weekend on Sunday evening. Sara became known as a "rink-rat" as she attended so many hockey games of her brothers. We met lots of great families and some of the young players and their parents remain friends of our family 50 years later.

My mother was a lifetime swimmer. She loved it in the water, and was still doing lap swimming well into her 80's. Early in the lives of her grandchildren, she was coaching them on the finer points of swimming and water-safety. Her home on Half Moon Lake in Eau Claire was just a few minutes walk from the city beach house, and the highlight of our visit there was to walk over to the beach house and swim the afternoon away.

The boys loved it, and when Sara came along, she did likewise. Mother's approach was to get the child acclimated to water very slowly, then as confidence was built, advance in very patient increments. The boys all became good swimmers. Sara began swimming competitively at quite a young age and continued through school, stopping only when she injured her shoulder swimming competitively in her third year of college.

Some of our friends from Church talked about a family camping experience at YMCA Camp DuNord on the shores of Burntside Lake near Ely, Minnesota. This began our experience with the beautiful Boundary Waters of Minnesota. A family camp with campsites, canoe instructions, short journeys into the wilderness to visit known camp sites, portages, fishing spots and viewing ancient Native American drawings (Pictographs) scratched on the walls of cliffs deep into the wilderness perhaps hundreds of years ago.

In the mid 1970's, we borrowed a pop-up tent camper from Uncle Charles and headed West to see Rocky Mountain Park, Pikes Peak, Banff and Jasper in Canada. A trip made more memorable by a certain bear who decided to enter our tent through a hole he made in the side.

We returned to the campground where our camper was parked after a day in the Hot-Springs of Banff and discovered the evidence of the uninvited guest. Before we left for town in the morning, I had advised everyone to be sure they did not leave food, candy or fruit in the tent because we were camped in an area of Grizzly Bears. Twenty-five years later Sara admitted she left a tube of toothpaste in the tent that day long ago.

The boys loved to fish and, in the early days, we would pack a family lunch and go to Lake Vadnais, just a few miles away from our Roseville home. Later, we purchased a new 14-foot Alum craft fishing boat with a 15 HP Evinrude motor and would team up with the Allison boys and the Bergstrom boys for a Minnesota fishing opener/camping out on Lake Milacs. Great times and lots of fish until the Walleye population went down as the fishermen population went up.

Then we rescheduled to beautiful Burntside Lake at Ely, Minnesota, where the Bergstroms had a new log home. Our all-time best fishing opener was catching ten Northern Pike weighing 77 pounds on opening weekend.

Steve loved baseball and played for several years in the summer league until he discovered golf. Mike played hockey until he was about 15 when he discovered Curling because of a friend who lived in a Curling family. He has been a member of the St Paul Curling Club since about 1980, serving as its President in 2015.

Sara was a competitive swimmer through High School and two years of college, when an injury forced her to retire.

COAST-TO-COAST STORES: 1976-1977

After eight years with Graco, in 1976, I got the itch for a bigger job and more money. The apartment building was doing fine and rents were coming in on time. I had also purchased 60 acres of hunting and recreational land near Talmoon, a tiny little crossroads in the wilderness of Northern Minnesota. I accepted the position as Distribution Center Manager with Coast-to-Coast hardware in Minneapolis. The company was a franchisor of 1200 Retail Hardware stores, many in small towns with "Main Street" addresses. All stores were independently owned with merchandise support, promotion, and retail store management services provided by CTC staff.

My job was to manage the Minneapolis warehouse operation serving about 500 stores in the Northern Division. This was a big job with a 400,000 square foot distribution center, and over 300 employees working under a collective bargaining agreement with the Teamsters. Multi-millions of dollars of consumer products inventory ranging from nuts, bolts and screwdrivers to garden tractors, ammunition and firearms were secure in the building. Coast-to-Coast was one of five large retail hardware store wholesalers headquartered in Minneapolis/St Paul at one time in the 1960's. The others, United Hardware (Hardware Hank), Our Own, Gambles, and Farwell Ozman Kirk (OK Hardware) were also servicing their stores in the Upper Midwest region with similar strategies.

My first big assignment at Coast-To-Coast was to provide the leadership to improve warehouse productivity and employee performance. The warehouse employees were working under an onerous Teamsters Collective Bargaining Agreement and the Teamsters threatened to strike every time the contracts would come up for renewal if they did not get their demands met. The business was being driven by its fear of Teamsters power to call a strike, a fear which had been causing management to consider many alternatives. A strike would shut down the entire group of five hardware distributors in Minneapolis and St. Paul leaving hundreds of small-town merchants from Kalispell, Montana, to Escanaba, Michigan, without merchandise for their customers.

Prior to my arrival, Coast-to Coast had engaged professional industrial engineers to study the conditions of all warehouse job functions to determine why the workforce overall was performing at a rate barely 60% of what might be a fair day's work. This group, led by a very competent Tom Zosel, began a study of every job and every function in the Distribution Center under every condition. They measured distance walked, weight lifted, number of items put away, items selected, full trucks unloaded, loading a tub or carton, packing and taping the carton as needed and hundreds of other functions of work in a warehouse. Working conditions in a Coast-To-Coast warehouse were near ideal. The place was clean, well laid out, fork trucks and hand carts were always available. Merchandise was placed on shelves, racks and pallets to make the inventory stocking and put-away work easy. Environmental conditions were excellent, breaks were convenient, and conditions for mid-morning and mid-afternoon stoppage for a smoke were timely.

My first year at Coast was a contract renewal year. The demands made by the Teamsters Union for a new contract were extreme. As usual, the demands, were expected to be met under threat of a walkout, affecting all hardware wholesalers in the area. This time, 1976, it would be different. Two of the large distributors had closed up their Minnesota distribution centers and relocated to Nebraska and South Dakota because of the caustic relationship with the same Teamsters group.

The negotiations for contract renewal of the Coast to Coast agreement began with an air of anxiety. The meeting was held at the Teamsters offices in St Paul. The Teamster's proposal presented by the "Business Agent" began with a demand to make every job in the building a "Premium Pay Position" That is: stockers, order pickers, truck loaders and fork-truck drivers, all of whom were well paid in warehousing circles, were all to be paid at premium rates under the new terms demanded by the Teamsters. Also, Company contributions to pensions were to be increased dramatically, "to take care of our people in their retirement." (It was not being said, but at this very time, the Teamsters and the Nevada gambling syndicate were being investigated by the US Government for being too cozy. Teamsters pension money was found to be supporting some casinos and mob bosses)

The meeting went on with demand upon demand. It was obvious from the contentment of the Committee attending, (all my employees), plus the Steward and the Business Agent, the demands being made of the company were meeting with their approval. When the "Business Agent" completed his list of demands, the Attorney representing the interests of Coast-to-Coast began to speak in a very straightforward way.

He informed the meeting in a calm voice that: "Today's meeting is not going to negotiate wages, benefits and working conditions of an on-going relationship ... but to negotiate the terms of a complete shutdown of Minnesota operations ... "We're relocating to South Dakota."

Now the room is silent! The observers representing the Teamsters were suddenly showing great anxiety. The rules being set down by the Company were: Hourly employees would be offered a cash termination settlement based on their years of employment. In accepting the settlement, they would forfeit all rights to follow the work and be employed by the company in any new location.

In the meantime, all working employees were to work at the new standards established by the Industrial Engineering people, which required an average increase in output of 40%. The "Standards" were challenged and later tested by an industrial engineering firm engaged by the Teamsters among claims that their "people" would be so overworked that illness and death may even occur.

The second opinion expressed by the outside industrial engineering study was that, **"The standards were fair and reasonable."**

The new facility was built in Brookings, South Dakota, located just over the Minnesota border on I-29 between Sioux Falls and Fargo. A new building of 400,000 sq. ft was under construction, rail spur was being laid, the State of South Dakota was giving tax breaks, completing access construction and providing funds for training all new hourly employees. The manager's job, my job, and all existing supervisors would be relocated.

An invitation was extended to all key employees to attend a big weekend tour of Brookings, visiting neighborhoods and schools, shopping centers, the hospital, the campus of the local University and attending a weekend college football game. The city of Brookings went all out to show the new transferees their town. Sandy and I, Mike, Steve, Dave and Sara enjoyed a college football game, a bus tour of all the city neighborhoods, schools, shopping centers and more that were featured. It was an all-out effort by the city to welcome us to the city they were very proud of.

The actual closing of the Minneapolis operation would be in the Spring of 1977. As a family, we concluded after much thought that we would not relocate. We had elderly parents in Wisconsin, deep roots in Minnesota and Wisconsin with our kid's schools, scouts, youth athletics, church and a large number of good friends. We had an investment in an apartment building, 60 acres of Minnesota hunting land, 80 acres of Wisconsin Recreational land and our new home, just a few years old.

The Company was understanding and requested I stay on-staff in Minneapolis to manage the last weeks of shutdown of the Minneapolis facility until the move had been completed., a request to which I agreed. My final project at Coast–to–Coast was to meet with the chief of the Minnesota State Police arranging for a series of off-duty State Troopers to be stationed along the route to be taken by truckloads of firearms and ammunition being transferred from a secure warehouse in Minneapolis to their new secure warehouse in Brookings, a distance of 250 miles.

This completed a Grand Slam. All five of the hardware distributors had now left Minnesota and the caustic labor climate of the area. South Dakota was a big winner with hundreds of new jobs and four new businesses with large payrolls and considerable real estate development.

Some of the terminating employees spoke to me in confidence during the shutdown. They did not like working with deadbeats any better than the company enjoyed having them on the payroll. The deadbeats were supported by the Teamsters who overlooked their destructive behavior to force the issue that more and more new employees were required to do the work. The unfortunate result was ... the entire group of 330 employees were terminated because of a few bad apples in the crew! The good news was some told me they were going back to school, others retiring, still others starting small businesses.

The Coast-to–Coast experience was good for me. I learned a lot from Lloyd Towner and Jerry Paar handling HR matters, Tom Zosel Industrial Engineering, Roger Stangland, CEO, Ken Hoffman Purchasing and Bob Gambill, my boss and Regional Manager.

AN IRRISISTABLE ENTREPRENUERIAL ITCH

By that Spring of 1977, I had been working as an adult for more than 20 years employed by the U.S. Air Force, Honeywell, Graco and Coast-to Coast Hardware Stores, each of which was a Corporate America institution. All had been great employers and extraordinary learning experiences. Now, I have just walked away from the biggest job of my career. Life in Brookings, South Dakota as manager of a 400,000 sq. foot distribution center with over two hundred employees was a big deal. How could I do that, Huh? I was 42 years old and had a streak of independence, perhaps the result of being the "only child" or, possibly "something else". I needed to learn more about something else.

At one time I thought of genetics as left-handedness, dimples in the chin, red hair, fair skin, tendencies towards certain illnesses, musical and mechanical gifts. Then, I began to think of other traits, which show up with human behavior.

I reflected on the lives of Arthur and Julia O'Neil and how they showed such **courage and decisiveness** in leaving Ireland in the mid 1800's. They were probably chased out by famine and cruel English landlords and were attracted to life in the USA because of a belief in **freedom and opportunity** for their family. But they left behind hundreds of years of family history and tradition, following their dream to the edge of the unknown in West Central Wisconsin.

Charlie O'Neil, my grandfather, son of Arthur and Julia, was born in 1872 when the family lived in London, Ontario had the genetic makeup including **independence** and **resourcefulness.** At age 18, in 1890 he acquired a textbook on Bricklaying and taught himself the lifetime trade. I have the book in my collection signed in his preferred identity "Chas O'Neil 1890". He was an independent contractor virtually his entire life and not quitting until he was 83 and dying of Cancer!

I thought about the enterprising Orr family and the **decisive** nature of their moves to the edge of the wilderness in Wisconsin in 1860. Maggie Orr O'Neil spoke of the Indian uprising frightening the pioneer families in the 1870's. Her family was settling on the edge of an unknown wilderness. Her Mom, my Great Grandmother, had the **courage** to travel with eight children, from the upper reaches of Maine to rural Polk County, Wisconsin, before the civil war, a trip of several weeks' duration.

And, Billy Orr, one of the eight Orr children to make the journey from upstate Maine, had the **resourcefulness and courage** in 1903. He founded an entire community and its local economic engine including lumber camps in the woods, a general store, a saloon, a hotel, a brothel and a bank. The village, Orr Minnesota, exists even today, 115 years later.

Grandpa Fred Bolier relocated his young family to Montana in 1910 and founded six businesses in a little prairie town, which even today is remote. Then, he and the family returned to the village of Baldwin, Wisconsin, and he found a way to create multiple new businesses and dominate the markets and trade areas in West Central Wisconsin with his brands, including "Bootleg Booze", "Bolier Beer Distributing Company", "Bolier Music Company" and the Bolier "Amusement Companies". That is a message not to be ignored.

I really had to look at the something else and I think I discovered a genetic factor linked to ambition, courage, risk-taking, personal decisiveness and independence. Life as an independent contractor is in my blood.

If there are Genetics leading to one having inheritances for starting new ventures… then I think I have a triple dose from the O'Neils, the Orrs and the Boliers. They were brave and courageous and decisive, and I am now believing some of that rubs off and passes on like curly hair, chin dimples and a propensity for conservative risk-taking.

My resolve was strong. Friends and colleagues from my earlier career were not at all surprised that I would find my way to doing ventures. So, ventures and adventures it would be for the next 40 years! I believe that behavior like that demonstrated by the early O'Neils, the Orrs and the early Boliers … can be inherited.

Chapter 6

THE RISE AND FALL OF THE ENERGY SHED VENTURE

THE RIGHT IDEA AT THE RIGHT TIME

My friend, Ted Bergstrom, had two engineering degrees, several published papers and several patents. Ted left corporate life leaving behind a high-tech job in a Fortune 500 firm to follow his dream of career independence. He was doing quite well with his home energy invention, the Thermograte, an after-market fireplace heat exchanger, which was unique and offered a rare but simple solution to homeowners seeking a secondary source of home heating. Ted found the customer motivation was generally driven by steadily increasing prices of conventional fuels being used for home heating. Homes in rural areas using oil or propane, as well as homes in urban areas using natural gas or all-electric were equally under price pressure and availability concerns. He observed the demand for alternatives was widespread.

Ted founded and ran the business from his garage, (like many other inventive startups) in the early 1970's. Since he was marketing by mail-order and speaking directly with customers, he had a great opportunity to compile market research on the needs and concerns of the homeowner. By 1977, Ted had expanded out of the garage and into a factory in St Paul and was ramping up a two-step distribution system with distributors and dealers handling Thermograte, the fireplace heat exchanger.

Now unemployed, I began to network for a new situation. Ted and I had been friends since the early 1960's. We had been on hunting and fishing trips and involved with our families in church activities. I valued Ted's friendship and his keen insight. He and his Production Manager at Thermograte, George Hegdahl, and I went to lunch at the Country Inn in Roseville, Minnesota. Both were very enthusiastic about the fast growing and ever-expanding market for their product, but quite willing to give me advice and encouragement in my job search as well. They suggested a conventional job search campaign using direct contact, networking, watching the classified help-wanted like a hawk and registering with an agent.

This, and future brain-storming sessions touched on many subjects, but one idea seemed to return to the mix. That was the concept of developing a retail outlet broadly assorted with residential energy conserving products. I had little retail experience except for janitorial work at Hollens during high school and two years during college working at Johnson Motors, a home and farm supply store in Eau Claire. I suppose my working for Coast-to-Coast Hardware supporting retail hardware stores was making its own contribution to my confidence about retail.

Little did we realize we were outlining a business plan for an alternative energy retail outlet serving the needs of the home-owner. In our brainstorm, "the store" needed a variety of products with supportable and technological benefits in saving energy or producing energy from alternatives. We considered insulation, windows and better siding as energy-saving products, with wood, coal, solar and heat pumps as alternative energy producers.

Sales persons and, ultimately, customers would require training in the processes of installing and obtaining the desired results from the products. I had grown up with a wood/coal stove in my house until I was about 10. However, I knew nothing about the world of Heating, Ventilating and Air Conditioning, (HVAC). Another friend, Paul Stegmeir, a Forester by education and University of Minnesota Extension teacher and Fire Safety Instructor by avocation, had the credentials. Paul was a savvy student of good forestry practices, residential construction and fire safety. Paul could design sales training curriculums and might possibly be interested in becoming a shareholder.

The concept needed an effective way to deliver products and services to the market. After much discussion, the warehouse with a retail front end seemed to be the answer. Merchandise vignettes to feature operating fireplaces, stoves and other functioning products would be beneficial to the merchandising strategy. The store needed an identity. A down to earth basic company name was required. We intended to sell solar and wind and support bigger and better residential energy efforts in new and remodel construction yet firewood and coal were the principle alternative fuels of the 1970's. The Energy Shed was suggested, I believe by George Hegdahl, and it stuck!

To give ourselves added confidence in our thinking about the public interest in energy products, we decided to attend an Energy Expo in Thief River Falls, Minnesota, in February 1977, sponsored by Ottertail Power. Ottertail was a public utility in Northern Minnesota. It was a very cold Saturday with lots of recent snow piles everywhere. The place was packed with the curious all day. George Hegdahl, my son Steve and I plus all other exhibitors were swarmed all day. To a pretty good degree, this event validated our thinking about potential markets and customers – at least in Northern Minnesota.

We paid lots of attention to national news regarding energy conservation and alternative strategies particularly for residential users. We did not know it at the time, but Washington was about to make a big move. In July 1977, President Jimmy Carter signed into law the formation of the US Department of Energy.

BUSINESS ORGANIZATION AND LAUNCH

George, Ted, Gene and Paul Stegmeir incorporated The Energy Shed, Inc. in the spring of 1977. We capitalized at $100,000 with $60,000 equity, $40,000 borrowed from the New Brighton Bank through Roger Sorenson, President. We personally guaranteed the bank debt. I was elected President, Paul, Vice President, Ted and George un-paid consultants to the new business. I set my salary at $18,000, far less than my Coast-to-Coast compensation, Paul accepted a reduction as well, thinking we could support our family obligations from savings and other resources for a temporary period. Ted and George would serve on the Board without compensation.

Sandy and I began to research for product. We tracked down Manufacturers and Distributors of products fitting our notion of our energy store. We attended the National Hardware Show and National Home Center Shows in Chicago and Dallas searching for products. We scoured the magazines and other publications serving the "Back to the Earth" bunch and Popular Science readers for possible products. We sought out well-engineered, safe and durable products.

Sandy typed out letters of inquiry to literally hundreds of manufacturers, their representatives and agents, distributors and dealers inquiring about the availability of their product for our new and different retail outlet. We were neither conventional retail, nor installing contractors, nor HVAC specialists, nor warehouse showrooms, nor fireplace decorators, but we were some of all of those. We became a curiosity and nearly all the companies we contacted came to see for themselves... and many liked what they saw.

Ted's product, the Thermograte, was the Cadillac product in the aftermarket fireplace conversion category. We were appointed a distributor and were purchasing in truckload lots within a few months. The Monarch Range Company in Beaver Dam, Wisconsin, the same firm that manufactured wood/coal kitchen ranges for grandma's kitchen for nearly 100 years, had a new product line. Their engineers had developed an add-on wood/coal-burning furnace to work in tandem with an existing forced-air furnace, giving the home a dual-fuel capability. They were impressed by our focus and appointed us a distributor. Within months truckload lots were arriving.

Majestic, a division of American Standard, appointed the Energy Shed a Distributor and gave us access to their line of Zero Clearance Fireplaces. In a short time, this equipment was being ordered by the truckload. LaFont Corp. of Prentice, Wisconsin, a hydraulics manufacturing company aligned with the logging industry of Northern Wisconsin, developed a line of high-quality log splitters. They appointed us distributor of their entire line, including a commercial log-harvesting machine for commercial firewood producers and gave us exclusive rights to sell the products.

Wood-burning stoves, some old established lines, some newly developed, were made available to us. The Shenandoah Manufacturing Co of Pennsylvania had 100 years of history selling to the Amish and Pennsylvania Dutch, and they made us a distributor. The Earth Stove and Gibraltar Stoves were of recent design. Their owners and senior managers were eager to have us show their line. The Kent stove from New Zealand, a parlor stove with a large glass window, enameled decorator skin, a secondary combustion manifold and approval from Canadian Standards (UL), became a big seller for us.

We were appointed a dealer for a solar hot water heating system; also, a DIY cellulose insulation blower and product system for the after-market. We brought in a line of weather stripping, door and window insulating products, added Husqvarna, and Homelite chain saws and Hunter ceiling fans all into our product offer. Manufacturers began to find us because of our unique approach to the energy savvy after-market. Locating new products got easier because the manufacturers viewed The Energy Shed as the leader in the residential energy conservation market segment.

The store was located in Roseville, Minnesota, in a warehouse building with a retail front end. Stegmeir had developed training materials for sales training in customer and employee clinics. He had slides of good quality installations, and of installations, which had gone wrong and caused fires. He put his stamp of approval on every product we featured.

The need for an informational tool to inform customers of the wide range of our products and applications became necessary. We chose a tabloid size, multi-page newspaper as the vehicle. Articles were authored by Stegmeir, myself and Ted Bergstrom. We featured articles on care and cleaning of chimneys, attic insulation and ventilation products, and safety first when heating with wood.

Accordingly, the first eight-page tabloid newspaper featuring articles about saving energy in the home, as well as energy alternatives in new or remodel construction projects, was published. With the aid of Bill Minnehan and Betsy Allison, Issue Number One was published in the late summer of 1977. Product ads in the tabloid paper were Majestic zero-clearance fireplaces; A high-efficiency electric hot water heater from Mor-Flow Industries; The "Little Gray Box," a water heater timer guaranteed to save $10.00 per month; The Nautilus Heat recycler designed to return warm air from the ceiling of the room to the floor; window quilts to stop drafts and 3M after-market window film to reduce glare and heat loss.

The paper featured Monarch companion furnaces, Thermograte, fireplace heaters, a complete line of weatherproofing products, Do-it-Yourself attic insulating kits and attic ventilating materials. Some manufacturers had co-op advertising dollars to support their promotional efforts, others had none, but if we felt the product needed a push, we featured it in our tabloid.

In July of 1977, we opened the doors at 1639 Terrace Drive Roseville, Minnesota. About 2,500 feet of show floor space. The show room featured several live-burning fireplaces, stoves, furnaces, solar water heaters, water-heater blankets to reduce heat loss and many other energy conserving appliances for sale.

Initially, promotional events were modest ads in the local papers. There was more store traffic from curious friends of the families involved than customers attracted by modest advertising. That was good, because we all needed practice and development of our sales skills.

THE GREAT MINNESOTA
GET -TOGETHER

The Minnesota State Fair is a big-league fair running twelve days and attracts well over a million people. We leased two adjacent booths, space of 200 Sq. Feet, in the Home Improvement Building at the Fair and expected to be busy. We ordered 25,000 newspapers and handed out nearly all of them. The Fair was a zoo. Wave after wave of people, eight abreast, came through and we had from five to fifteen customers in our booth at all times. The crowds were steady from 9AM to 9PM, and it continued for twelve straight days. This was an incredible kick-off of a new business concept addressing the homeowner concerns for energy conservation in their homes.

We were short of staff, obviously, but ... George Hegdahl, an imposing 6 ft 3, 375 lbs. mammoth man stood in front of the booth beside a glass door model of the Thermograte and, in a booming voice, spoke in glowing terms of the assets and features of the Thermograte for hours on end. George would attract so many people to his presentation, the aisles were plugged up. Paul Stegmeir, also a large man, had a cluster of prospective customers surrounding him looking at, into and around our Monarch add-on furnaces, a hot water boiler and several of our firewood processing tools, including hydraulic wood splitters. Young Mike and Steve O'Neil were fast becoming Thermograte salesmen and had their share of customers. Even Eadie and Jack Allison were working the booth. Sandy and I were floating and answering multiple questions, placing an Energy Shed News in everyone's hand and pointing out the store location just two miles North of the Fairgrounds. "Come visit our store, where all our products are on full display and operating."

The Fair ran twelve days, twelve hours a day and launched the Energy Shed. We had opened in July and the cash sales were very slow, which was good, because we all needed time to learn the products. After the fair, it was booming. I was already at 14-hour days. We needed more help. My old buddy, Bill Bonesho, came in to handle buying, inventory and warehouse management; Eadie Allison came on to handle office; wife Sandy to prepare us for our first computer for inventory management; Mary Donahue to help in the office and on the sales floor; Jon Kusske to manage the retail store; Tom Berglund to assist in the retail store; John Bonner, at 80 years and a forty-year background of selling Monarch Ranges, was back to sell Monarch add-on furnaces; Father Frank Kenny, launching a new career in retail; and Al Sevald, a "rock," in the store. My old Eau Claire friend Bob Neperud also came on board to help.

Willy Farbelow, sons Mike, Steve and Dave, Bruce Rehwaldt, Andrew Arnold and others were handling warehouse duties. Merchandise was flowing inbound in boxes and cartons initially, soon thereafter in full 40,000-pound truckloads. Everyone worked long hours. I was in by 6:30 AM, home by 6 PM, back to the office by 7 PM and home by 11PM almost every day of the week. Bonesho took over purchasing, which lifted a load off me, but would soon change because of growth.

The Board had formed the business in April 1977 with cash investments of $60,000, supporting an additional bank line-of-credit of $40,000. As outside interest in our concept grew, it was obvious by June we may have a business with growth potential and projected cash shortages. I had held back some cash for back-up if needed but was looking for alternatives in outside financing. One day we had three semi-trucks preparing to unload full trailer-loads of product on our dock and orders in our office for virtually all of it to ship within days. I thought, now that's a way to make money in merchandise sell-through.

I began to look hard at franchising as a business expansion strategy in that first few months of the business. My intuition was that we needed a transfusion of additional financing before long and the founders were tapped out. When we began the business, we arranged for outside accounting to include audited financial statements. In the event we decided to franchise, or in the event of a public offering at some time, the rules for each required audited financials.

FRANCHISING

As owners/investors in the "The Shed" our personal financial resources were limited and should we not be able to generate sufficient cash quickly enough, franchising would be an alternative method of supporting growth. The founders did not have the deeper pockets needed, we did not have an angel, additional debt was out of the question but franchising has merit ... if we can persuade others to join the flock!

Under that form of business, the Franchisee supplies the financing of inventory and start-up expenses, secures the lease of a suitable property, prepares the property for business and hires the staff as necessary. The company, the "Franchisor", supplies the license to use the trade-mark, and trade secrets, the training and procedures for operating and marketing, the channels for merchandise and the know-how of operating the business for which it (the Franchising Company) is entitled to certain fees and charges. Franchising is a common method of business expansion in the retail hardware store business, fast food and hotel/motel businesses. My recent employer, Coast-to-Coast Stores, was a franchisor of 1200 hardware stores.

During the spring and summer of 1977, we were finishing up the legal work leading to a registration of an Energy Shed Franchise Offering. My mentor was Vern Vanderweid, a brilliant attorney with the Weiss and Cox law firm in Minneapolis. Vern was a graduate of the Geo Washington University, College of Law, the school of many U.S. Government attorneys. Among other things Vern was a law clerk in the office of Gerald Ford following his graduation. He was incredibly savvy regarding the laws of Securities Offer and Sale in the USA. The franchise laws were as complex as the laws to offer and sell stocks and bonds to the public and Vern was our guide through the maze. In addition to the SEC rules, the State of Minnesota and several other upper Midwest states had additional rules to apply to the offer and sale of franchises.

Vern and I spent many hours molding the Energy Shed Franchise offer to meet all the Federal and states rules. We must have done it right because we sold 15 franchises and never had a contract issue with the SEC, the States Departments of Commerce or with the consulting attorneys of any of our franchisees.

Little did I suspect that the one-on-one training I received from Vern during this time would become an important foundation to the franchise consulting business I was to begin several years later.

By Fair time in August 1977, Bob Jonason, my old boss at Setchell-Carlson, had swept up the first Energy Shed Franchise ... to be located in Lindstrom, Minnesota. In the following two years, we opened fifteen more new stores with owners who shared in the "Vision". We were open In Fridley, North St Paul, Bloomington, Duluth, Brainerd, Cottage Grove and Rochester Minnesota. Also, in Fargo, North Dakota, and Rapid City, South Dakota. Eau Claire and Appleton, Wisconsin. We opened, Lombard, Illinois, and Webster Groves, Missouri, all parts of the growing "Shed System".

We would assist in site location and lease terms. Stegmeir would bring in the owner, spouse and sales people for 40 hours of intense classroom training as well as live training on the sales floor. On-the-floor sales took place as one-on-one, the classmates would sell each other on the products selected.

Following training, the opening order of merchandise was shipped to the store for the owner to unpack, assemble as required and prepare the sales floor for operating and demonstrating equipment. By the time they had completed the unpack, assembly-as-needed, read the owner's manuals and built model vignettes in their store, they were getting close to opening the doors to a real live customer.

We made trips into stores periodically to visit with the owner, notify them of new products coming along, or suggest advertising or merchandising ideas proving successful in other stores. Annually, we would hold a week-end meeting with all stores invited. Product conferences, success and failure stories were shared, industry news and our interpretation of the state of energy industry was shared.

I was the principle franchise developer and franchise Operations Executive. Stegmeir did all the training and product knowledge work supplemented by Ted Bergstrom on Fireplace conversions and heat loss calculations.

The company fiscal year closed in December,1977. Though doing business only from July through December, sales tallied up in excess of $500,000 in 1977 dollars. The launch was above expectations in sales and traffic and a bit terrifying, since we were not equipped or staffed for this level of business. We had opened the bottle and the escaping genie was an 800-pound gorilla!

We had a notion that seasonality was at play and the likely business curve would bulge in the third and fourth quarter. We predicted that home remodeling, new home construction and especially lake/seasonal home installations would be very active in the spring and summer months in the upper mid-west states. We adjusted inventories a bit, rebalanced staffing and focused on growth ideas, including franchising.

THE FIRST FULL YEAR

During early 1978, the world press continued to raise the estimates of fast escalating energy prices and simultaneously periodic shortages from interrupted supply lines. Oil reserves were slipping and prices were increasing. The notion of oil prices at $50 per barrel going to $100 by 2000 was frightening.

The Shed marketing program began a new radio program with Stegmier and radio personality Chuck Lilligren with a weekly one-hour show on Minneapolis St. Paul AM WCCO, 50,000-watt clear channel radio. This was a program aired as a public service in a time slot of 5-6PM on Sunday, usually just following the Sunday NFL game.

Stegmeir was getting bookings to speak before wood energy members, fire safety personnel and county and state associations. Washington was rumbling about energy tax credits for homeowners installing insulation and solar equipment, Congress was seeking answers, as were many states. Our business model was attracting interest from many places in the USA and abroad. Two businessmen from Utah arrived at our place in Roseville. They showed a great deal of curiosity and level of understanding, quite beyond most of the people we were speaking to about franchises. It was mentioned they were close to the LDS church in Utah and were observing our business to acquire knowledge for un-specified purposes. (I presumed, since the LDS church has a fetish for self-sufficiency, they were researching our little venture.)

Another fellow came in specifically to see me. He was an employee of Royal Dutch Shell headquartered in London and was at our place to understand what we were doing with product and services. He asked for no more information than a typical customer of the store or prospective Franchisee, so I was not in any danger of leaking trade secrets. We had attracted the curiosity of his company because, in his words, "The energy problem in Europe is much worse than it is in the USA". Further, Royal Dutch Shell, which was one of the largest oil companies in the world, would look to working partnerships or outright acquisition of concepts to transport to Europe. He was in my office on two separate occasions but nothing more ever came of it.

The strain on our cash was severe. Between much larger inventory investment in our inventories and our receivables growth, demand on cash was painful. We were turning inventory at a rate of 8 times per year, very excellent for most businesses, our margins on sales ran about 40%, also very excellent. On this basis, we began to bump our bank line, but unfortunately the prime rate was increasing quickly and we were borrowing at 1½ percent over prime. With the velocity in inventory turns and holding margins, we were ok with the bank and serviced the debt but some long-term financing would be required soon.

In order for Sandy and me to stay above the waterline, I sold my Graco stock acquired on an option, sold the St Paul apartment building, sold the 60 acres of hunting land near Talmoon, Minnesota, re-financed my home twice and exchanged my son's college funds for Common Stock to support the inventory and receivables demands. My partners were unable to increase their investment. I was seeking venture capital and working my way around Minneapolis where these investors were located. The show-and-tell menu was to meet our people, read our tabloid newspaper, review our Franchise-Offering Circular, analyze our financials and visit our stores. I repeated the drill many times.

Sales in 1978 were $1.4 million and a high concentration of sales were in the third and fourth quarter. We definitely had a high seasonal component to deal with. We sought out alternative counter/seasonal products and began to sell chemical (waterless) toilets for our remote cabin owner customers as an example. We rejected winter sports and spring gardening categories as being too incompatible.

REACHING OUT

ABC (American Broadcast Co.) called and requested an interview to air on their coast-to-coast radio network. Later, Radio KSL of Salt Lake City, called to schedule a one-hour interview, which was broadcast in the evening through their 50,000-watt clear channel radio network. (My cousin Bonnie Curtis' husband, an over-the-road truck driver, was driving through Wyoming at the time and listened). Articles about the company appeared in Money, Business Week, The Boston Globe, San Francisco Chronicle, Minneapolis Tribune and Corporate Report. All seemed to have curiosity about the business and its progress.

I received a phone call from an office in Washington inviting myself and Mrs. O'Neil to attend a five-day national energy conference to be held at a conference center on Chesapeake Bay, just outside of Baltimore (and DC). The conference was sponsored by The Aspen Institute for Humanistic Studies, the Energy Productivity Center of the Carnegie-Mellon Institute, the Franklin Research Center and the US Department of Energy. Chaired by Senator Bill Bradley of Massachusetts, this was a high-powered conference and we were invited to attend, all expenses paid. (Our first vacation in two years)

The conference was being held in a very classy place and reeked of big government facilities and big Eastern money! It was stunningly beautiful, and well appointed. Conference attendees were lodged in private cabins scattered throughout the wooded conference grounds. Sandy has just completed reading the novel "Chesapeake" and was struck by the many geese in the bay, the museum and artifacts on the grounds. The five-day meeting was held some part of each day in the main conference center, a large room with a very large round table without a podium. Everyone at the table was treated as an equal participant.

When Senator Bradley asked for those at the table to identify themselves, Sandy and I were the only people at the entire table of 40 who appeared to be facing customers and making a living at selling energy stuff! No one appeared to be schlepping products or meeting customers except us! They were all on someone else's payroll, with a larger mission including the US Government, The Carnegie Mellon Institute, The Aspen Institute and the University of Pennsylvania among others. It was a memorable occasion. Five days at a very exclusive resort conference center on Chesapeake Bay – a big deal for two kids from Eau Claire Wisconsin hacking out a start-up business.

Our story was getting out. The Minneapolis press picked up on us and a few articles were printed in the Tribune and in Corporate Report, the magazine for the 9th Federal Reserve District. Somehow, I believed that by sharing our story we would attract the attention of a venture capital person. Our financial condition was not good. The prime rate of interest was increasing at an astounding rate nationally, and we were borrowing at a rate 1½ percent over prime!

Some suppliers were having trouble producing sufficient quantities of merchandise at the rate our customers were buying. Sales of some wood energy products were lost, but we added lines of merchandise from new qualified sources to replace them. Some sources of wood stoves were as far away as New Zealand.

Sales ended the year of 1979 at $2.6 million. This was not a break-even rate of sale; however, we took a degree of comfort in the fact that we had quite a small loss. Though, most of us were continuing to work at rates well beneath our street value.

THE SHED GOES PUBLIC

In March 1980, the New York Times published a half page article on the company in their business section. In an interview with the local reporter I advised the company was a start-up but was showing leadership in a very narrow industry segment. Not long after the New York Times article was published, Jerry Alstead of Alstead, Strangis & Dempsey, a Minneapolis securities underwriter, called. He was aware we were searching for working capital and thought he might be able to help. Jerry was very curious and spent many hours in discussions about the four founders, our employment records and business backgrounds. He studied our stores and observed our engagement with customers.

In the three years of the Energy Shed business operation including 1977, 78, and 79, leading up to the year of the public offer, total revenues were $4.5 Million. The company was capitalized with just $60,000 of equity and $40,000 in debt in 1977. In the course of business during the three years we had increased our line to $400,000 at 1.5% over, prime and we the principals were on the hook to guarantee it. I personally invested another $23,000 in cash from refinancing my home, selling a parcel of hunting land in Itasca County, Minnesota, selling common stock in Graco and investing my son's college fund, all in exchange for 40,000 additional shares of the company in my son's names.

After serious study, Jerry made a proposal to underwrite an Initial Public Offering, (IPO) of Energy Shed Common Stock. He proposed a plan to offer 1,500,000 shares of Common Stock, par value $0.05 and requested 150,000 additional shares as an over-allotment option, all at 1.00 per share. The proceeds were to be used (1) to repay short-term bank indebtedness guaranteed by the Company's Officers and other short-term indebtedness, (2) to pay trade vendors and to repay other accounts payable (3) to pay off obligations incurred in the acquisition of capital equipment and to relocate the office and warehouse facilities.

The company had incurred operating losses during its formation and ramp-up over the three years of $202,000 on sales of $4.5 million in the same period. From a start-up in mid-1977, the loss of $200,000 was a relatively modest amount. An examination of our inventories and accounts receivable would reveal what happened to the money.

In preparation for going public, two additional members were recruited for the Board of Directors. Chuck Mencel was a friend from Eau Claire and CEO of RayGo, a manufacturer of heavy construction equipment. Bob Ashbach, a friend of both Bergstrom and the O'Neils, was serving in the Minnesota Senate and had a banking and construction background.

The legal preparation for a public offering of common stock was extensive, as were the legal hoops for offering franchises. Again, we called on our attorney, Vern Vanderweid of the Minneapolis firm of Wiess and Cox to assist in the preparation of the company and the documentation necessary to offer and sell common stock in the public market. Vern was very patient and was a teaching attorney for me again since this was my first time through the State and Federal Securities and Exchange Commission (SEC) rigid standards for an Initial Public Offering, (IPO). When all the questions had been addressed, the project moved forward. The stock was offered at $1.00 per share and opened on the market at a premium of $1.50 per share. The entire issue sold out, including the 150,000-share over-allotment option. The Shed team was happy, the underwriters were happy, the banker who had approved the expanded line of credit was happy.

The cash after expenses amounted to over $1.3 million dollars. The company debt was retired, removing the obligation of the Energy Shed Officers to guarantee the debt further. All accounts payable to equipment suppliers were paid. Merchandise invoices and other miscellaneous payables were paid. The warehouse and offices were relocated to a larger warehouse in Little Canada in advance of an expected record sales year. Leasehold improvements were completed, and the company had a reasonable amount of working capital for the first time.

ROCKY TIMES

Stegmeir was getting antsy to further his profile on the national wood energy stage. He had become a popular speaker at national conventions of the Wood Energy Institute and the National Fire Protection Association. He was frequently published in national trade magazines and his reputation was large nationally. The national stage was a good fit for him, and we were fortunate to have had him as an investor and officer in the formative years. Paul left the business.

Steven Frederickson joined the Energy Shed team and assumed many of Paul's training and product selection duties. Steve came from a family with roots in the heating business. He was well educated and had a very practical and hands-on talent for home remodeling and up-grading. He was an owner of a number of residential properties. Steve became our technical go-to guy.

In early 1981, the federal prime rate of interest hit 21½%. That was a signal for most Americans to stop all plans for home remodeling and new home construction, the very motivational factor of most of our larger retail sales. In January, "Black Friday" hit the Energy Shed Office. We received cancellations from franchise stores for nearly $400,000 of booked business at their stores. The company store in Roseville had an identical experience with many cancellations of customer orders with deposits down and deliveries scheduled.

FHA home improvement money was virtually unavailable or at 22-23%. It was so expensive, customers just shut down plans to remodel. And, with mortgage rates over 20%, new home starts came to abrupt halt. Our buyers had ramped up orders to meet this expected inflow of business. We had truckloads of stoves, fireplaces and furnaces on order and some even on the road to us at the moment we called in our cancellations.

Some purchases were stopped and cancelled. Others, we accepted if the company would give us extended dating. We gave the stores longer discounts if possible, and we offered "warehouse specials" for firm orders with early payments. Over the next weeks and months, the stores, and later the public in Minneapolis/St Paul, were invited to "warehouse clearance sales" with big discounts offered. One of our builder customers decided to promote his sale of new garages with a free Solar Hot Water Heater system so we moved some inventory to them and got paid.

To lower costs, we terminated a number of our people. Unfortunately, we had relocated to a larger warehouse/office facility in Little Canada having a fixed lease cost considerably higher than the prior space.

In 1981, Ronald Reagan became president. The Reagan Administration began to place very serious pressure on the "energy industry." As if by magic, new methods were found for discovering and retrieving oil from fields thought dry. Drilling rigs, which could be sent down holes in the earth and on command, make right angle turns towards more oceans of oil. Within a year, new drilling techniques, new fields of oil were being discovered all over the world. The Mid-East, the North Sea and South America, The Canadians developed technologies for extracting oil from sand. And North Dakota was discovered to be sitting on an ocean of oil. The OPEC nations got the word ... produce or else! And by 1982, President Reagan was able to call the world energy crises something other than a crisis, it was an oil-rich world again with proven reserves sufficient for many years!

And then ... we just scrambled every day for sales and cost reductions. It was an exhausting and heartbreaking time for all.

DOWNSIZING

In 1982, sales were tough. Some of the franchise stores were calling it quits. Appleton, Brainerd, Fargo and Lombard were all in trouble. Duluth, Rochester and North St. Paul were doing better. Just after the IPO, the bank debt was retired, bills were paid and inventory in the warehouse was owned. A year later, the bank line of credit was opened again. It hurt to do it!!

My personal life had been to apply every ounce of energy I had to the business. From day one prior to opening the first store, I had been on extended hours and very focused. Long days were required, partially because we were always short of staff. Now in 1982, the staff was reduced even further and the load was spread a little thinner.

Frederickson and Bergstrom were becoming great confidants. They were kind enough to not mention my mental health but I hurt. My savings were gone, I thought 60-hour weeks were a vacation, I had to let my old friend Bill Bonesho go, and I feared the whole business was coming apart. I was broke, could not sell any more of the family assets to raise cash, could not refinance the house again, bank and venture financing was out of the question. I was beat. Sandy had been there every step, and she was discouraged and frightened. We had a family of six, no money for fun stuff, no vacations, our net worth was virtually gone and we're nearing age 50.

Every year we were in business, Roger Stangland, President of Coast-to-Coast stores would keep in touch with me. Roger was complementary about my management of the CTC warehouse operation. He would stop by to look over our new store and visit for a while. Roger was a first-class retail executive and I was always flattered by his interest and curiosity in our venture. About 1978, he was promoted to Executive VP for Household International, Corp. the parent company of Coast-to-Coast Hardware and Ben Franklin Stores, both franchising businesses. He was also responsible for Von's, the California Food Store Chain, and TG&Y stores, a large corporate-owned variety store chain. Together, I would guess there were 5,000 total retail outlets in his domain.

I placed a call to Roger in mid-1982 when things were very low. I informed him I needed a job and would appreciate his guidance. I knew the Brookings job was in good hands because I had recommended Dick Spiegleberg, my assistant in the Minneapolis facility, but Roger was well connected and was a great contact for me. A few weeks later, I got a call from a Ben Franklin VP. Ben Franklin was a sister company of Coast to Coast. We chatted a bit and he said he was having someone from Ben Franklin call me to arrange a visit. One thing led to another, and I became a candidate for a Regional Manager position with a Vice President title to match.

I appointed Steve Frederickson to my job, and by now it was a very tough turn-around with slumping sales and fixed costs eating away. Steve was up to the job, whatever was required. And, what was required was to shut the doors in 1983 and liquidate the assets. The Shed had taken its toll on me, as well as our family, I was broke and broken hearted, Sandy was scared but supportive. Mike, Steve and Dave were emancipated and finding their way. Mike was enrolled in a photography education program, Steve attending college in Eau Claire, and Dave started a tough assignment loading UPS trucks at night and U of Minnesota days, and Sara still in high school. Sandy and I were starting over, but the Shed was behind us and at least out of sight.

THROWING IN THE TOWEL TO MY DREAM

I suppose everyone who experiences a business failure has lots of remorse. We were beat up but not dead! I was exhausted and my partners and our families were as well, victims of ambition to breathe life into this dream and unwilling to accept the fact we were under-financed from the beginning. I under-estimated just how big the demand was for these appliances and how well our business model was positioned in the market.

As it was, we sold thousands of appliances in this seven-year period and brought a new level of awareness to thousands of families on the matter of conservation of precious natural resources and energy alternatives. We were so close to the edge. In our first three years we created a market for $4.5 million sales (in 1977 dollars) and lost just less than $200.000. Possibly a better financed venture could have weathered the storm but we were unable to keep our people and keep the doors open.

Though I lost my shirt, my "small business savvy" had increased dramatically. Sandy was very worried about our future, our near complete financial train wreck and what we were going to do. I told her we will leverage the past experiences into a more savvy Gene O'Neil, Business Consultant and push forward. She bought it! Without boasting I believed the losses we suffered in savings and net worth could be replaced in 5-10 good years of earnings. My answer must have been persuasive.

Chapter 7
OTHER OPPORTUNITIES COME KNOCKING

BEN FRANKLIN STORES

I put the Shed in the rear-view mirror and began work for Ben Franklin in late summer of 1982. I joined the Franchising and Real Estate Department in the Minneapolis region, one of four regions within the company. I was furnished a car, worked alongside two experienced real estate and store development fellows, John Evans and Clair Flaten, attended all the meetings and attended one large company meeting at the HQ in Chicago.

By early 1983, I was in-training at Ben Franklin HQ in Des Plaines, Illinois. There would be a position at the VP, Regional Manager level for me within a few weeks. I was living in a Corporate housing property, a fully furnished apartment, in nearby Des Plaines and commuting home on weekends to prepare the family for relocation.

In April, I was named Vice President and Regional Manager of Ben Franklin's Central Region, headquartered in Seymour, Indiana. The Central Region contained 400 Ben Franklin Stores in Indiana, Kentucky, Tennessee, Ohio, Michigan and Illinois. I left Chicago and reported in at the Regional Office in Seymour, Indiana. My predecessor was on his way out the door.

The company had arranged housing for me at a furnished corporate apartment in Columbus about 15 miles from Seymour and a nicer community to live in than Seymour. Columbus is where we purchased a newer country home, three miles out of the city on 7 acres. I was furnished a new 1983 Oldsmobile sedan, a comfortable office in the same building that housed the regional warehouse, a good compensation plan and a staff of 15 experienced retailers and field sales consultants. The field sales people assisted the 400 stores in our region in matters of merchandising, local promotion, competitive strategy and lease matters. Each was responsible for 35 stores in the region, plus we had a store planner and a craft trainer, two finance people and two store set-up people.

My job was to assist this staff and store owners in business management issues. This was a big job, made bigger because Wal Mart was expanding rapidly from their base in Arkansas, and spreading like wildfire. The facts, when they were finally understood were, Walmart was crushing Ben Franklin. Store count in Kentucky and Tennessee in earlier years was well over 150 stores in these two states, when I arrived the store count was down to 16 stores total ... in the two key states.

Sandy and Sara moved down in July to our charming new country house on seven rural acres outside of Columbus, Indiana. The three-car unattached garage had an upper story for storage and a roof like a Wisconsin Dutch barn. The July day we moved in, the temperature was near 103 degrees, about normal for Southern Indiana in July.

My weekly schedule included four days of travel per week to visit stores to render an opinion on marketing or management matters and visit with struggling owners experiencing tough competition. The most frequent concern was the Walmart steamroller. The average Ben Franklin Store at the time was 5,000-8,000 sq. feet, on main street or in the newer shopping center at the edge of town. The store was filled with a variety of merchandise including toys, office supplies, fabrics, patterns and sewing products, house-wares, modest priced apparel and more. The average store was family owned, often by a couple who shared the selling and merchandising work.

It was not uncommon for the family to have lived in an apartment above the store in the beginning. The family was involved in the church, school, Lions club, PTA, morning coffee with the pharmacist, the dentist and the owner of the nearby motel.

In the days before Wal-Mart, the family could make a living, buy the building, pay off their home, work hard for 30 years and sell the store to a new owner and retire to the Ozarks. The average trade area for a small BF Store was 10-30 miles in small town rural America with farm families and small-town residents being fiercely loyal to "their" local store.

Sam Walton had owned 22 Ben Franklin Stores in Arkansas in the 50's. In 1960, he visited the Chicago headquarters of Ben Franklin and urged the company to develop a large store format with extended lines of variety merchandise, pharmacy and groceries. In its questionable wisdom, Ben Franklin senior management, at the time, chose to ignore Sam's advice, so he did it his way!

In 1962, Sam opened his first Wal-Mart store in Rogers, Arkansas, the same year Dayton-Hudson opened their first Target discount Store in Roseville, Minnesota. When I entered the scene in 1983, there were Wal-Marts all over my territory and a new 1.0 million sq. ft. distribution center located in the same Seymour, Indiana, where our offices and warehouse were located. We learned the Wal-Mart business strategy of the time was to find a county seat community with a trade area of 10,000 people, open an 80,000 sq. ft. Wal-Mart store and price all existing merchants out of the market. The local variety store, pharmacy, gift and card store, hardware store and soon the grocery store were soon destroyed.

Store-owners under siege reported their sale circulars and tabloids featuring their best specials would be posted on the Wal-Mart store bulletin board with the prices circled and a lower Wal-Mart price hand written onto the circular. Through 1983 and 1984, my team worked hard to assist stores with strategies to develop business with or without Wal-Mart in their town. Some stores had merchandised more heavily in crafts and games, in fabrics and patterns for the home sewer, in custom picture framing, in locally made consumer goods and in services which Wal-Mart did not provide.

In 1984, I realized the utter hopelessness of the Ben Franklin Owners. The Wal-Mart thrust was massive and overpowering. Owner-operated Ben Franklin stores could not overcome the steamroller of the corporate giant. I began a quiet campaign to locate a new job, hopefully in the Twin Cities. We missed our family and our friends back home.

RETURN TO COAST-TO-COAST

Coincidently, Senior Management at Ben Franklin and sister company Coast-to-Coast, stores, both under the Household Merchandising umbrella, agreed to co-develop a new retail concept to be placed in select markets to combat the overpowering thrust of Wal-Mart. With my experience in both companies I was selected to join a small venture staff to develop such a concept and to open several test market stores with interested franchise owners. Coast-to-Coast was selected as the lead company and my friend Lloyd Towner, VP of Human Resources at Coast hired me back into the Coast family to be domiciled in Minneapolis to develop this project. Our relocation and moving expenses would be paid by Coast to Coast. A fabulous stroke of luck for the O'Neils!

Once again, Sandy, Sara and I were relocating – this time back to Minnesota. A very happy day! I reported to Coast-to-Coast in Minneapolis in the fall of 1984 and lived in the Radisson South Hotel for ten weeks until Sandy and Sara could return in January at mid-term break.

The new Coast/Ben Franklin store was to feature the best lines of both company programs. Since Wal-Mart was not strong in professional grade power tools, we would be. Since Wal-Mart did not repair windows, cut pipe, or service small engines, we would. We intended to assort the store by choosing product and services, which did not directly collide with the nearby Wal-Mart store. It was a tough call.

The project adopted the name "General Store," created a distinctive red/white décor scheme and a prototype store plan layout in 15,000 sq. ft. The first store was in a Ben Franklin location in Jackson, Tennessee, east of Memphis. The second prototype was set-up in a Coast-to-Coast store location in Northern California. I was traveling every week to one location or another to supervise the changeover.

Sandy and Sara were making plans to sell the Indiana house and move our goods in early 1985. Since I was working from Coast-To-Coast Corporate offices Eden Prairie, Minnesota, we began to shop for a home to buy in the western Minneapolis suburbs. Several attempts to find neighborhoods to suit our lifestyle forced the decision to return to the more comfortable Shoreview area where we had lived and our family had grown up.

Blaine Edmundson, our home-builder from 1969, was interested, and he found a lot suitable for the house of our vision. Sandy, Blaine, and Blaine's draftsman began to design the new house. Since we would be empty nesters in a few years, we decided on a walk-out rambler with all primary facilities on the main floor, including laundry and master bedroom. Construction would begin in January and the home would be complete in May,1985.

We needed short-term housing in the Mounds View School District where Sara would attend high school and our new home was located. My expectations were in locating a property similar to those Corporate Housing pads I experienced in Chicago and Columbus, Indiana, during my 1983 relocation I searched for furnished apartments, condos, or homes with a six-month or less lease. Throughout the north suburban area, I found only a tired, worn-out and stinky apartment building on Lexington Ave with a one-year lease. There was nothing else, and it occurred to me that this was a business venture waiting for someone to develop.

Several Fortune 1000 firms were located within a five to seven-mile radius of the area. Control Data, Medtronic, Cardiac

Pacemakers, Land O Lakes, Deluxe Check Printers, 3M Company, St Jude Medical, Schwing America and several others were all fast-growing firms in the area and all prospects for interim housing for employees being relocated. I made a mental note regarding the business opportunity I smelled here.

I still needed housing for Sandy, Sara and me in the Mounds View School District for four months while our new house was under construction. A new condominium property was being developed in the North Shoreview neighborhood of Royal Oaks, just a few blocks from our new home site. They featured a ground floor, 832 sq. ft, 2-bedroom unit with a single car garage at $2,500 down and a $46,000 mortgage at 6.5%. It suited our interim needs and had promise as a short-term rental unit, should we decide to pursue that venture. I bought one unit, and we moved in enough furniture to get along for four months. With a new home under construction and a new townhouse for the interim period, I turned my attention to the new job of developing "General Stores" to do battle with Wal-Mart.

However, another surprise ... in early 1985, ownership of Ben Franklin and Coast-to-Coast was changing. The new General Store concept was being scrapped, because the two firms were no longer sister companies under Household International ownership. Each firm was coming under the ownership of new firms. My job was going to require relocation to Denver, Colorado to which I said "Thanks but no thanks".

I resigned ... and left Coast-to-Coast for the second time ... now at age 50, ... without a job, but full of self-confidence.

We had moved into our little condo and re-connected with our family and friends. Mothers Cozy and Florence, each climbing into their 90's, were very happy to have us back in the area. Mike,

Steve, and Dave, all of whom stayed in the Twin Cities during our absence, were a great help in reconnecting. Presbyterian Church of the Way friends, plus the Sieverts, Allisons, Bergstroms, Seversons, Neperuds, Sandy's book club and our Eau Claire gang of Losby's and Hansons, were all on our re-connect list. We slipped back into circulation easily. Sara began at Mounds View High School and reconnected with some of her old classmates, swimmer athletes and friends from her elementary days at Turtle Lake School. We were back in the neighborhood and intended to stay!

HANGING OUT THE SHINGLE, AN INDEPENDENT CONTRACTOR

My 30 years, including four in the military, as an adult wage earner, had been a magnificent learning experience. I assembled a portfolio of lessons learned ranging from employment in small, common service businesses to high technology at the edge of space and world admiration, from small business to Fortune 1000. I was an able employee always with an ambition to achieve. I was nearly always the first one in the office in the morning and the last to depart in the evening. For years I believed ten-hour days were normal and a couple of hours on Saturday were to add the extra touch as needed. I was known as a high achiever and self-motivated.

It is only a few years after the Energy Shed experience and I am out of a job at age 50. For many years I had been telling myself that self- employment was where I wanted to be and this might be the time. My domestic responsibilities were in order. Our marriage was sound, our family was nearby, friends were close, our new home and neighborhood were beautiful and we were both healthy!

FRANCHISE FORUM, INC.

In early 1985, I created and registered my new trade-name, "Franchise Forum," and began to network throughout the Minneapolis /St Paul Area. The Entrepreneurs Network, was a group of people of many different stripes, ranging from small business owners to service providers, accountants, attorneys, bankers and aspiring top and mid-management people. Monthly meetings over lunch with presentations on law, marketing, distribution and plenty of time for mingling was the basic format. I obtained several referrals from these events and found I was able to attract interest from a number of varied businesses.

I was prepared to sell my services an hour, a day, a week, a month or more at a time as an independent contract employee specializing in Franchise or two-step distribution company development. I had wide experience and a few scars to show for my past efforts. The very facts that I had created and launched a franchising business and taken the business to the level of an IPO went a long way in persuading prospective clients to talk with me.

The real bonus was, I had lived through the disclosure of every paragraph and component of the franchise offering as well as those for the IPO, the Initial Public Offer of the company common stock with the securities-savvy attorney, Vern Vanderweid, of the Wiess and Cox law firm as my mentor.

Work to stimulate my independent consulting business began rather quickly. For example, a prospering Native American community with a very successful casino on their hands had interest in franchising other Indian communities. This successful group felt their know-how, proprietary games and business operations could be replicated in other Native American communities. I did not get the job, but they did successfully expand their business practices through other means.

The owner of two specialty retail shops asked for assistance in re-positioning "Kafte" and "Kitchen Window" for growth and perhaps franchising. The cost estimates to franchise frightened the owner, but he thanked me for my candor and paid for the advice.

The owner of a specialty cosmetics retail store asked for advice on improving sales through merchandising. She was operating in a high-traffic location in an enclosed mall. I worked with her and made recommendations leading to a 40% increase in sales per sq. ft. in a high-traffic shopping center and no increases in fixed costs.

The Elna Sewing Machine distributor in Minneapolis hired me to write and publish a dealer manual. Sandy and I authored, and Sandy published the manual. Our compensation included a high-tech computer driven Elna electronic sewing machine from Sweden.

I was asked by a family to advise them on franchising a business they called "Gentle Transitions", a service assisting elderly folks who needed a little help transitioning from their home into senior housing. At ages exceeding 65, my advice to these owners was to not take on franchising at their age, because the financial and emotional demands are exhausting. They paid for the council and thanked me for the careful analysis.

Paper Warehouse, Inc., a privately held Minnesota-based party store chain, needed assistance in the development of a franchise program to accelerate growth of their business. With my assistance they grew to a chain of 124 stores, both corporate and franchised. Later, I was hired by Air-Vend, to develop more business from national convenience store chains. Air-Vend manufactured coin-op vacuums found at car washes and rest room vending machines for personal products with sales and service provided by licensed area dealers.

Insty-Prints, Inc., was a Minneapolis-based franchising company of 160 quick-print shops in markets ranging from Montana to Michigan. The stores were known for one-color printing and fast turn-around photocopies. My two-year engagement was to assume the VP Marketing position and develop the programs to elevate the service-offer the franchised stores made to customers.

My team reorganized and upgraded all the marketing and advertising tools used by Insty-Print stores. Included was a distinctive new four-color logo, which created an up-tempo identity for the stores. We also developed a 24-page, full-color catalog of product and services rendered by the local stores and an updated, direct-mail program managed by our staff to do creative and contract laser-like mail services in trade areas served by the stores. Our creative person developed a point-of-sale lobby graphics series to dress up the largely drab front ends of the stores.

St Thomas University hired me to teach an evening course on small business development to evening extension students, all of whom were aspiring entrepreneurs.

Deluxe Corporation, a Fortune 500 firm and the largest check printing firm in the country, was losing market share to up-start printers and a huge loss of business to electronic funds transfer. I proposed a "hub-spoke" solution for Deluxe in which printing for small business customers was completed at existing remote Deluxe printing plants. We entered into an 18-month contract to develop the proto-type. The Hub/Spoke business concept was adopted and expanded by Deluxe several years later.

NORTH SUBURBAN INTERIM HOUSING

This venture was launched in June 1985 by Sandy and I simultaneously with the completion of our new home and launch of the Franchise Forum Consulting practice. We outfitted the townhouse we were living in, to test and evaluate the "Short-Term Furnished Housing" business concept. The property was in the Cherrywood Hills Condominium Association, a newer 96-unit condominium property in residential North Shoreview.

We knew most "Corporate Housing" properties were located in the more commercial areas such as I had experienced in Chicago and Columbus, Indiana. We suspected a residential setting such as our Shoreview location would be satisfactory for temporary housing for transferring singles or couples with one to two children. This proved to be an assumption that was "right on".

In 1986 I was recruited to be on the condominium Board, and a year later was elected as President of the Homeowner Association, a position to which I was re-elected until my resignation thirty years later.

The business concept required careful planning and tweaking initially before we stuck our neck out too far. We continuously searched out our competition and were prepared to adjust our product if necessary. Advertising and promotion included newspaper and direct mail using a list I had carefully created.

Direct contact to meet contractors, corporation relocation specialists, real estate relocation specialists and cold calls on real estate developers and contractors was a part of the early marketing campaign. We measured our responses carefully and noted any enhancements, which might be recommended. We measured the costs and returns from each segment, made changes in furnishings and pricing and our rental policies as appropriate. Keep it clean and simple and provide smothering good service was our goal.

In 1988, with three years of experience, the test was doing very well. We were turning away rentals each month so we acquired two more units for rental, increased rents and they too were rented and flowing cash immediately. In 1990 we assisted Son Dave in the purchase of his first home, which was another condo unit identical to our rentals in the same Association complex. Later, Dave asked if he could join with us and expand the service further with more acquired properties. We created the partnership DASAGON sharing profits and losses 50/50 and acquired three more units making an overall group of six properties in the marketing group by 1993.

The business plan was successful when measured by positive cash flow every month since 1985! Because my consulting business was also flowing cash, all cash produced by the rentals were applied to retirement of the mortgage(s). This snowball effect allowed us to pay off all of the mortgages and become debt-free in the property rental business by 2003.

This meant Sandy and I could now take a deep breath and start enjoying life a little more as we looked forward to our retirement.

Chapter 8

THE JACK PINE HILTON - OUR FAMILY DEER HUNTING RETREAT

DEER HUNTING – A FAMILY TRADITION SINCE THE 1880'S

In Wisconsin, Deer hunting is extremely important to many families and has been a tradition of the O'Neil's since the 1880's. Though originally there were no season limits and no license requirements, modern deer hunting began in the 1930's with limits, and an official season. The deer-hunting season is the third week of November, over Thanksgiving.

Living in Wisconsin, one would learn that very cold weather sets in about this time and frequently snow is on the ground, but 500,000 - 600,000 or more hunters take to the woods in hopes that they will get their buck.

My dad had been hunting deer with his dad, Charlie, since about 1918. Their first hunting camp was located just south of Superior, Wisconsin. They had an old Army tent from WW1, set up the tent on public property and hunted for several days. In the 1930's, they upgraded their hunting digs. They would take along a roll of tar-paper (roofing paper), find an abandoned cabin or farm building in rural Polk County and move in. *(Note: during the Depression there were many foreclosed properties left by people who could not pay their taxes)* They would nail the paper on the inside of the structure to close off the drafts, set up a small wood heater, two bunks, a kerosene cooking stove, kerosene lanterns, and hunt the nearby woods for several days.

In 1946, Dad and Grandpa Charlie, who still lived in St Croix Falls, bought an 80-acre parcel of wooded forestland in Sterling Township. They purchased the 80 for $250 plus back taxes of about $60. Sterling Township is the area where both the Orr and the O'Neil families homesteaded in the 1860's and 1880's.

During the Great Depression (1930's), when taxes on the land were $6 - $9 per year, the owner of this property was unable to pay them and the property was foreclosed by the County. Charlie discovered it in 1946 as foreclosed county property and he and my Dad bought it in 1946. The property measures 80 acres, two 40-acre parcels on a dirt north/south road with woods in all directions except west where lower ground and Cowen Creek flows. It's mostly level ground, with trees, trees and more trees. It's as primitive as it was when the Arthur O'Neil and James Orr families moved into the area as pioneer settlers in 1860's and 1880's. At that time, Native American families were living just six miles northwest of this property.

The acreage is fully wooded with Jack Pine, Poplar, Birch, Maple, White Pine, White and Red Oak trees. It became the Deer hunting, Grouse hunting and winter recreation land for the family. As an added bonus, the property produced wild Blueberries and Raspberries in season. It's buried deep in the woods of Polk

County, Wisconsin, north of St Croix Falls where it's primitive and remote even today in the 2018 period.

Across the road to the West of the cabin there lies a large grassy wetland, a mile or more wide, which runs North for twenty or more miles. This wetland was once a large producing area of wild Sedge Grass, a product used in the manufacturing of floor coverings before the arrival of linoleum. There were two factories located in the swamp to process the crop into floor covering. This grass was used by the Native Americans of the area, for basket and mat weaving.

The roads in the area are still dirt but plowed of snow in the winter for the convenience of hunters and others using the area for recreation.

There are no utilities into the area even today in 2018. Cabins are heated with firewood, oil, or propane. Cabin cooking and lighting is supplied by propane, there is no indoor plumbing – the "biffy" is out the door and into a small and unheated shed.

"THE SHACK"

In 1946, Charlie and my Dad with help from Uncle Red Norwick erected a hunting cabin on the property using walls reclaimed from an old tool shed in Grandpa's back yard in St Croix Falls. They added a roof, a window, a floor, a kerosene lantern and a Coleman lantern for light, a kerosene stove to cook on, a small wood heater and two military bunks for beds.

We called it simply "The Shack." It was 8 feet by 8 feet by 8 feet tall, ample enough for two hunters for a few hunting seasons.

The first addition in 1948 would triple the space inside when they built a room addition of 8x16 feet, on an east/west line directly behind the original 8x8 structure. My dad's folks, Maggie and Charlie, thought a lot of Uncle Red and he and my Dad were as close as brothers. They truly enjoyed hunting, working on the cabin, playing cribbage and harvesting firewood. Also, Uncle Don Bolier, my mother's younger brother, was home from the war, and he, too, enjoyed the Shack and hunting.

In 1959, a new kitchen wing and wood shed were added. In 1978, a larger room was added across the front of the cabin to accommodate more hunters – for sleep, eating and recreational card play. After its most recent additions the cabin is quite spacious by cabin-in-the-woods standards possibly 900 square feet. We have bed space for 13 and table space for 13, but outhouse space is still limited to one at a time. The seat never cools off.

Water is abundant, but none is on the surface. In the 1980's, our deer hunters were drilling a new well. As we drilled down, we found good water at about 26 feet. Drilling the well was easy because there were no impediments to our drill. There were no rocks, stones or gravel in the entire 26 feet, just this fine sugar sand.

I remarked about this to a fellow at the Polk County offices who told me the sand ranges from 70-700 feet deep, depending on location, in the St Croix River Valley. This is the valley of the St Croix River, a major outlet for drainage of Lake Superior as the last glacier melted 10,000 years ago washing down millions of cubic feet of fine sugar sand. It's this same sand that was so discouraging to the early settlers who discovered the soil unable to support reasonable agricultural crop growth.

SIX GENERATIONS OF HUNTERS

November 1954 was my first hunt from the Shack. I was 19 and home from the Air Force on a Thanksgiving leave. I did not shoot a deer, but dearly enjoyed my two days in the woods with my dad and uncles Red and Don. Unfortunately, Charlie O'Neil had died in July, but I recall we toasted him with a swig of beer.

My dad taught me how to run a chain saw safely and split and stack cords of firewood, how to respect the woods and practice good fire safety rules. I learned early that Red or White Oak wood, which was dry and hard was the best for fires in the stove. We harvested oak trees felled by wind or disease as our principle source of firewood and always had a woodshed attached to the cabin, one half of which was full of fully seasoned firewood and one half of which was the wood harvested and drying for next year's use. Virtually all the firewood came from recent dead falls in the woods behind the cabin a few hundred feet.

My children, the fifth generation to enjoy the woods of Polk County began visiting when they were very young, possibly age 4. Each of them probably has a favorite story to tell of a visit to The Shack with their grandpa in the 1960's and 70's. For a couple of years, the boy's Boy Scout Troop came up and set up a little village of pup-tents on a wooded spot 1/3 mile from the cabin, close, but very remote in some dense woods reeking of adventure for young boys.

A walk in the woods was always therapeutic for me. Whether alone or later with Sandy, sons Mike, Steve, Dave, and then Sara, a walk in the woods was good for the brain. In the woods we find pretty flowers, and interesting trees, mushrooms, and tree lichen, big trees and little new trees, broken old trees, a running deer, a Porcupine up a tree, Ravens and an occasional Bald Eagle.

On one memorable walk in the woods with Mike, when he was about 10, (the early 1970's), we discovered a place deep in the woods with near cathedral-like beauty. Three massive White Pine trees stood like pillars from an ancient building. We estimate the trees to be over 100 feet tall and nearly four feet in diameter. Because these woods had been heavily logged off in the 1880's and 90's, these trees must have been left as a symbol or somehow were memorialized by the loggers. The spot has been a favorite hunting spot by our hunters since our discovery.

Nick, Dave's son, the sixth O'Neil generation to prowl the woods with his Dad, began hunting when he was 13. He is good in the woods. Dave has taught Nick to hunt with a bow, as well as with a gun, and he enjoys both. When Nick was about 15, he had a nice streak, three deer with three bullets! I think the whole family of hunters would applaud Nick on that bit of hunting prowess.

STORIES AND LEGENDS FROM THE CABIN

In 1960, my Dad began keeping a "journal" at the cabin – making entries onto a calendar hanging in the dining area of the cabin. On every visit he would record the weather of the day, the sightings of critters including deer, bear, coyotes, porcupines, martens, fishers and more.

He recorded the names of everyone who arrived to join in or just to chat. When someone came to dinner, they would be added, as well as those spending the night. He was like an inn-keeper in a remote village.

Since his radio was always on, he would note the score and winner of whatever game he might listen to that day. Twins, Brewers, Packers and Vikings, U of Wisconsin or Minnesota scores were recorded. During the hunting season, he recorded the sightings and obviously the kills, if any, during the seasons. Those records are saved, all of them since 1960.

My Dad loved and respected the woods and the cabin. "You do not kill a tree unless necessary" "Always be careful with fire in the woods". "A clean and freshly painted cabin is a happy cabin"; "Every bed is made with clean sheets"; "Scalding hot dish-water and rinse prevents the "Screamers"; "We only shoot what we intend to eat" (except for destructive varmints); "No drinking in the woods" and "never a loaded gun in the cabin"!

The cabin was his get-away. After his retirement maybe 50-60 trips a year he would drive up there, always with a project to do. Painting, cleaning, fixing, adding on-to or bringing up a new whatch-a-mah-call-it. Since his original home was St Croix Falls, he had many friends and families in the area to visit. His Sister Carol and family Paul and sons Neil and Jay live just a few miles to the west in Lindstrom, MN so quite often he would take a side-trip over to Lindstrom to visit.

So many of our favorite people have been there for an hour, a day, a season and, in some cases, many seasons. My friends, and I'll likely forget some but: Charlie and my dad, Gene Sr, Grandma Maggie and my mother, Florence, Red & Evie Norwick, Don Bolier, Uncle Vic & Aunt Hazel Mallongree, Aunts Edith Nelson and Marge Gavin, Uncle Paul & Aunt Carol Norelius, Ted and Vi Norelius, Uncle Mike and Aunt Peg Heebink, Cousin Tracy Nelson, friends Tom Hanson, Bill Bonesho, George Losby, Jack Allison, Eadie, Sue, Betsy & John Allison, Ted Bergstrom, John and Bill Bergstrom, Bruce Rehwaldt, Steve Pater, Kelly Whitwam, Rick Berken, Cousins Neil, Carla and Jay Norelius, Brad and Brian Norelius, cousins Marilyn Heebink/Stutt, Nancy Heebink/Mason, Georgia Heebink/Clausen, and Gail

Heebink/Skinner, Sandy's brother Dennis Tietge, Sister Cheryl Tietge her mom, Cozy, and her Aunt and Uncle Charles and Maryellen Miller. Old Honeywell friends, Harland and Joy Sievert and Energy Shed colleague Steve and his wife Jeanette Frederickson, came for ski and snow-shoe days. These have made the memories of life at the cabin in the woods unforgettable.

The cabin décor includes the antlers of many deer our hunters have taken from the nearby woods, a few babes on calendars from years long past, carpet on the floor recycled from my aunt's motel, a double bunk to sleep 4, another to sleep 3, another to sleep 1, an old army cot next to the wood stove and one tiny bedroom for whomever is currently paying the real estate taxes.

This primitive little cabin in the woods has been a place for serious daytime hunting with no drinking allowed during the day. At nighttime, card games and a selection of adult beverages (with the Manhattan cocktail being the most popular) is standard evening fare. The Manhattan is created with two measures of Canadian Windsor Whiskey, one tiny measure of Martini and Rossi sweet (Red) Vermouth, a dash of bitters and one cherry on ice. If there are no bitters, forget about it, if no vermouth, forget it, no cherries, forget it and just drink the whisky over ice.

In the early days all those staying for the night were invited to taste Rattlesnake Meat as an appetizer and take a swig of blackberry brandy as initiation to the ways of the North woods.

(Note: On the 6th of October 1975, my Dad's 70th birthday and fighting Cancer, he wanted to go visit the deer camp. He and my mother and I drove up from Eau Claire. He was only able to drive the first 20 miles then became too tired and surrendered the driving to me. He died on November 14, 1975 and was buried in the Baldwin Cemetery on Thursday November 17. In a graveside ceremony the burial and service took place in an

advancing snowfall with wind driven by a stiff 40 MPH gale from the North. It was/was not a coincidence that he was buried on this day. His habit for 30 years was to go get the shack ready for deer hunting on this Thursday, the day before the Deer Hunting season began. When we, the hunters arrived on Friday evening the cabin was warm, the beds were made and the beer was cold. He was well aware this October 6 was his final trip to the "Shack.")

Gourmet dinners have been served here. Wild duck from Aunt Carol and Uncle Paul, and many venison dinners by our camp cooks beginning with Charlie and my dad and, keeping up the tradition, my sons Mike, Steve and Dave. My dad, and Grandpa Charlie before him, prepared a very fine "Booya" always about the third or fourth day of deer camp using the leftovers from meals served earlier in the week. They always added Rutabaga, a (Turnip like) root vegetable with history going back to Ireland. Eating at deer camp was always an event, often featuring venison, roast beef, ham or Pork.

Jack and John Allison served Eadie's lasagna, to hungry hunters, Uncle Dennis Tietge created a memorable chicken soup and for many years has supplied delicious chocolate turtle candies to the camp of hunters. Bruce Rehwaldt brought pickled eggs and peppers, Steve Pater a delicious hot hamburger dip. Sandy O'Neil has made a chile for at least 60 years of hunting parties. My sons Mike, Steve and Dave, all good eaters and good cooks never fail to make camp chow memorable. Regardless of the weather or the hunter's success ... we always eat well.

An Uncle Don Bolier story from the 1950's that is a part of the legend needs to be told. After the war, Don was taking all the service calls from the family amusement games business. No cell phones at the time, so at 4:30 each day after hunting, he would drive into Cushing, find a phone and call home in Baldwin where the family would have accumulated the service calls for machines in need of repair. If urgent, he would go to the place and repair the machine, then come back to hunt the next day.

This particular evening, he drove to Spring Valley, repaired the machine, ran into some of his friends and they all decided to go to South St Paul for dinner. Somehow over the evening, there was a police raid on the place and Uncle Don was arrested for carrying a concealed weapon. He was carrying his hunting knife on his belt and a hunting shirt concealed the weapon, thus his arrest. He was released late that night with charges dropped. When we all got up in the morning, we found Don asleep in his car in the front yard of the cabin. He did not want to wake us by coming into the cabin during the night.

Then, there is the tale of old "One-Tooth", an imaginary character of renown, who hangs out at the Wolf Creek Saloon during deer season inviting men to buy her a beer. The young and the uninitiated hunters in our camp are advised that deer hunting is a serious business but if "One Tooth" begins to look good it's time to go home.

Our most consistent game producer has been Steve Pater (Allison son in law) one whom we believe has extraordinary tree climbing instincts and a nose for the critters. His camp record ten-point buck was taken several years ago soon after he and the Allison boys began to hunt with us.

Next, probably son Dave with great patience though son Mike has been a frequent producer, Nick O'Neil is on a fast track to be a fine hunter. The all-time record deer hunt was in November 1988 when six bucks were shot opening weekend by the camp hunters. Another memorable event was a certain season in the 1980's when hunter Ted Bergstrom learned his Cancer was cured … he shot three bucks that year.

I shot my all-time record buck on November 27, 2010, a twelve-point 150-pound buck. Steve Pater made a European mount of the head, which still hangs in my office. Grandson Nick shot a ten pointer the same day.

In the 1970's and early 80's, we had family weekends in the woods in February and March. Snowshoes and cross-country skis were our means of getting into the woods. There was something quite comforting about being in the quiet woods with two feet of snow on the ground. Finding a place where one could grab a seat on a log, build a fire to warm up the hands was a memorable event. Some of the ladies were not fond of the cold seat in the out-door biffy, but as far as we know, no one suffered badly.

Other non-hunting visits are to cut firewood for the cabin as well as our home stoves and fireplaces. A group of 6 or 8 of the hunters and friends of hunters will gather in early October with chainsaws, hydraulic log-splitters, pick-up trucks, an off-road vehicle, large and small trailers for a firewood cutting episode. We take no live trees only those which have died or tumbled in a storm. When complete, the cabin woodshed is full and several pick-ups and trailers are loaded for the trip back home with enough firewood to bring charm and heat to our recreation rooms all winter.

A number of years ago one of our imaginative hunters, we believe the credit goes to Jack Allison, renamed our humble place, tongue in cheek, the "Jack Pine Hilton." It was a fitting name, and so the "Jack Pine Hilton" it has been ever since. Jack was a hunter among hunters, died from cancer way too early, left an indelible mark on all who knew him. Jack, Ted Bergstrom and myself, with our boys, had a record of over thirty consecutive years of father-son hunting, fishing and camping trips with our sons.

Chapter 9
RETIREMENT - DOIN' IT "OUR WAY"

MY UNFORGETABLE GOLF SAFARI

When I retired in 2000, I wanted to celebrate big and asked others if they cared to join Sandy and I on a Golf Safari. Some years earlier, Sandy's Uncle Arthur and Aunt Carol, both avid golfers, had ventured around the world playing golf in many lands. I wanted to do something like that but with certain limits.

I invited our family and golfing friends to join us for a Friday evening of turkey dinner from the Weber grill. Thirty-two showed up. The next morning, Saturday, we launched the safari with 28 golfers on a course in Wisconsin, just east of Stillwater, Minnesota, followed by dinner at a great steakhouse in Hugo, Minnesota. Day two on Sunday, we played New Richmond, Wisconsin, and more than 20 of our golfers played. Day three on Monday, twelve of us convened at another beautiful course, Turtleback, in Rice Lake, Wisconsin, finishing up in late afternoon as a storm was brewing with big rain and high winds.

The storm hit just about the time we had all finished golfing and arrived at our lake house near Birchwood, Wisconsin where we would spend the night. Winds were near 70 MPH from the west, temps were high 80's, rain was heavy, we're all in need of showers and ... the power goes out. There is no hot water for showers, no power for the electric stove, and no water for washing or bathing since our well required electricity to operate the pump. Candles, Coleman Lanterns and flashlights were used until power was restored. We brought up enough buckets of water from the lake to flush the toilets and wash the hands and face.

Dinner was prepared on a Coleman Camp Stove by master chef, Sandy's uncle, Dr. Arthur Miller. The storm passed later, but power had not been restored when it was time to eat and later retire. Everyone had a place to sleep. Three bedrooms, plus a sleeping loft with a hide-a-bed and inflatable double air mattresses gave everyone some comfort.

In the morning, more golf, now with just eight hard-core golfers remaining from our safari group to play the local favorite, Tag-a-Long. Power was fully restored, and then we were on our way to Ely Minnesota, where we would spend the night at the Bergstrom log lodge on Burntside Lake and play the Ely Country Club on the following morning. However, a storm hit the Bergstrom lake home that night and their power was out. In the morning however, we would play the Ely Country Club. "Billy-goat hills" they call it.

The last course on our Safari, with only four of us remaining to play, including Uncle Arthur Miller, Ted Bergstrom, Bill Bonesho and myself. We played Giants Ridge at Biwabik, Minnesota. This may be one of the top five public courses in Minnesota. It's beautiful and challenging.

Those of us remaining had played seven courses in seven days, a total of 126 holes. The courses were all handpicked by me, and I think everyone loved it as much as I did.

THE JOYS OF RETIREMENT

Sandy had spent the last several years of her working life at St John's Hospital in Quality Management. She retired in 1996 as our family financial situation had improved and her appetite for new challenges had increased. Her retirement was an exchange of hospital work for volunteer work, grandchildren, two book clubs, church jobs including a stretch as Deacon and Funeral Coordinator. She is a fastidious housekeeper, homemaker and holiday home decorator. She has been a lover of classical music, and for 30 years has had season tickets to performances of the Minnesota Orchestra, one with a world-class reputation. She takes great pride in never going to bed in an unmade bed! She is an addicted crossword puzzle addict and a very loving grandma to Becky, Katie, Madeline, Nick, Megan O'Neil and Sandra Jean Fish.

Over the years, she held grandkids day-care for Madeline, Nick, Megan and Sandy Fish. She taught them colors, alphabet, numbers, table manners, toilet matters and how to read. She played goalie for Nick, age 5, as he shot tennis balls into an imaginary hockey goal-mouth. We took the kids on short trips to see The Dalles of the St Croix, and Crystal Cave and the zoo and Como Park in St Paul. She taught the art and the craft of holiday Scandinavian baking to the grandchildren, and every holiday season they gather to make breads, rolls and cookies of many kinds. She has a reputation throughout our family, friends, acquaintances, renters, postmen and paper deliverers for producing the absolute finest holiday peanut brittle.

I retired at age 65 in 2000, comforted in our financial recovery from the train wreck after The Energy Shed. I wrapped up my last consulting project in 2000, and Sandy and I were determined to do some foreign travel. My retirement had been mostly busy with property management duties, both on our own account and as 30-year president of the Cherrywood Hills Condominium Association, a 96-unit property. I read mostly historical stories of WW ll and early Irish history. I golf weekly in a Senior men's league, meddle with family history and have been the Chair and chief organizer of my high school class reunions the past five years.

I have hunted deer for 65 years – missing only one year when I was recovering from hip surgery. I was a respectable league bowler for about fifty years, holding averages in the 175 range, and had a career best series of 666 and high game of 240. I am a veteran blood donor – having exceeded five gallons some time ago. My golf game is respectable, but always leaves me challenged to improve on average scores in the range of 94-104 for 18 holes.

In the autumn and long winter, I am a firewood junkie. I harvest hardwood from the forest, taking only dead or storm damaged Oak trees. I cut, split, transport and carefully stack to allow 1-2 years of seasoning of up to four full cords of firewood. During the cold winters of Minnesota, I maintain a wood fire in an efficient wood-burning stove for about 16 hours each day. Firewood cutting, splitting, transporting, stacking and burning is recreational and therapeutic for me!

OUR LAKE HOME

A home or cabin at the lake is highly prized by us in the Land of Lakes. Sandy and I had looked forward to a time when it might be possible for us and 1993 was the time. We purchased a modest three-bedroom cabin on Red Cedar Lake near Birchwood Wisconsin between Rice Lake and Spooner. The cabin was newer but modest and was within our price targets. The ½ acre property was fully wooded, on a blacktop road with low traffic. The nearby areas were heavily wooded and housing density was low. The lake was well known as a lake for Walleye, Smallmouth Bass and abundant pan fish.

The lake amenities were stunning with nearly ten miles of water to explore, great views of sunsets and an abundance of Bald Eagles, Osprey and Great Blue Herons to observe. Family or friends would visit nearly every summer weekend. Sandy and I were there nearly every weekend in the summer and one or more weekends per month in the winter. The place was heated, insulated and very cozy. Several nearby golf courses, the Ice Age Trail, the Blue Hills of Wisconsin, Rice Lake, Spooner and numerous out of the way resorts and small-town saloons with delicious Friday Fish Fry dinners were all on the agenda for our choosing.

In 2000, just after my retirement, we contracted for a total remodel, which included expansion in all four directions and straight upward with a 20 foot "Chalet" front. When it was completed, we had wall-to-wall windows and floor to ceiling windows. Summer or winter we had the sense we were outside while still inside because of the windows. Inside we placed an abundance of Knotty Pine planking including in the ceiling of the great room overlooking the lake. A loft overlooking the lake was added and grandchildren thought that was to coolest place to claim as their own.

We cruised around the lake, fished and partied on a 22 ft pontoon boat. We loved the place and received many kind comments from family and friends. The place was so nice we were spending virtually, all our leisure time there and missing out on other ambitions including travel. In 2008 we sold the lake house at a nice profit, retired all our debt and made plans to travel.

TRAVEL TO IRELAND

We have visited the home village of the Arthur and Julia O'Neil family of Cromane, County Kerry, near Tralee. It's nestled between the Dingle Peninsula and the Ring of Kerry, a very beautiful area in Southwest Ireland. The Atlantic Ocean is just one or two miles away. On a recent trip, I gathered a handful of the soil and two stones from this property and returned to the USA to place them on the gravestone of Arthur and Julia, buried in the cemetery at Wolf Creek, Sterling, Polk County, Wisconsin. Then I gathered a handful of the dirt from the exact location of their pioneer home in Wisconsin, which I will deliver to their farm site in Cromane on my next visit.

Beyond Cromane, we have seen quite a lot of the Irish island, its rolling hills and "farty shades of green", and its miles of limestone (Lace) walls separating farmer O'Neil's property from farmer Donahue's. We have seen the sheep and cattle browsing in the fields and responsible for the green as they recycle its nutrients. The villages are charming. With the removal of the automobiles from their streets, they retain the charm of the Irish community of 200 years ago.

The mighty Atlantic crashes the western shores in a futile attempt to erode the substantial Basalt outcropping anchoring the island to mother earth. On the bluff at the Cliffs of Moher 700 feet above the sea, some claim you can see Boston when standing on your tippy toes. We have seen the sun set on Galway Bay and the Irish Musician Bono on the streets of Clifden. We marveled at the courage of Alcock and Johnson in a flight from Labrador to Clifden long before Lindberg hit Paris.

We observed Eddie Doherty weave Donegal tweed on a 200-year-old hand-loom in Ardara, north of Donegal. And, two years later, Sandy purchased a shawl with Eddies label from a shop in Hayward, Wisconsin. We have seen Beleek China in production and in the hands of the artists with the most delicate touch. We have seen the artists at work on Waterford Crystal turning sand to the most beautiful and artistic glass art.

In the walled city of Derry (Londonderry) and at Donegal Castle, we discovered the O'Neill clan had been very engaged in the life of Northern Ireland from Donegal to Derry and Co. Tyrone in the 1600's. They left their mark. We have seen the North Atlantic at peace with the North Shore of Ireland where rollers hit the sandy shoreline in a gentle, repetitive and rhythmic way.

In Belfast, we have toured the museum of the magnificent Titanic, which was built to an elegant standard for the well-to-do of the day yet failed to reach North America on its first voyage in 1912. We have seen the Book of Kells in Dublin, the Guinness Brewery, the historic, but not very pretty, River Liffy, the statue of Molly Malone, Kilmainham Gaol (the paupers prison) and Waterford Crystal in production.

On a cruise to Alaska several years ago we became acquainted with other passengers Kenny and Heather Moore whose home is in Coleraine, Northern Ireland. We have lodged with them in Ireland where they have been the finest of Irish tour guides, very knowledgeable about interesting sights the tour busses miss. On their visits to the states we have shown them the bluffs of the Mississippi river separating Minnesota and Wisconsin, during fall color change, also Duluth Harbor and the North Shore of Lake Superior.

Kenny tells the story of Finn McCool, a legendary Giant, who crossed the 12 miles of ocean to Scotland on the Giants Causeway to see his girlfriend. Kenny scoffs at any geological nonsense regarding the origin of the Causeway.

TRAVEL TO EUROPE

We have visited the sobering sites of and near London, scarred by the Battle of Britain, including Churchill's war rooms, Eisenhower's war planning rooms, the Hurricane and Spitfire air bases; and the inspiring Cliffs of Dover. We have seen five Normandy Beaches and cemeteries where thousands of soldiers' bodies from the USA, Canada, England and Australia lie. We traveled France, Luxemburg, Germany, Austria and the Netherlands as well as stunning Nuremberg and Cologne in Germany on a trip of a lifetime on the Danube and the Rhine rivers.

We have visited Prague in the Czech Republic and Budapest, Hungary to Bucharest, Romania on the Danube River. All show the effects of the Communist influences over many years. And, all may take another 50 years to heal.

TRAVEL TO SOUTH, CENTRAL AND NORTH AMERICA

We have cruised around South America visiting Chile, Cape Horn, the Falkland Islands, Montevideo, Uruguay and Buenos Aires, Argentina. A later cruise to Panama, Central America and

Mexico followed still later by a cruise to Alaska and the west coast of Canada. We have visited Denali Park in far Northern Alaska and the city of Ushuaia, in far Southern Argentina. Each, just a few hundred miles from their respective poles. Standing on a tall ladder you may be able see their poles.

TRAVEL THROUGHOUT THE STATES

We have seen all 50 states including Alaska and Hawaii. We know and love the Midwest the most. Wisconsin and Minnesota, land of forests, farms, rivers and lakes bordered on the north by great Lake Superior, on the East by great Lake Michigan and loaded with mighty rivers, forests, agriculture and outstanding people. We have visited the largest cities in the Country and many small and quaint towns as well. New York, Los Angeles, Chicago have been visited. Gnaw Bone, Indiana and Exira, Iowa have something in common ... American families and pride.

THE FAMILY – PASSING DOWN THE GENES

Our first son Mike left the hockey but never the ice. He continues as a lifetime Curler and is past President of the St. Paul Curling Club. He was educated as a professional photographer and has been employed by Best Buy.Com for many years in their product presentation lab preparing the images we see on-line at Best Buy.com. Mike's wife Susanne is employed by the national ladies' cosmetics firm Aveda in the advertising and product promotion area as an editor of sales, advertising and promotional materials. Susanne has a Master's degree in education. Their daughter, Madeline has completed a semester at Limerick University in Ireland and earned a Bachelor degree from the U Wisconsin, Stout and will go on with graduate work in Children's

Occupational Therapy. The family has extensive camping experience including remote Canada, Minnesota Boundary Waters the Rocky Mountains and more recently have been exploring Ireland and Scotland by car.

Son Steve, earned a Bachelor degree from U of Wisconsin Eau Claire and an MBA from St. Thomas U. He specializes in the marketing and sale of sophisticated diagnostic equipment in the practice of dentistry. He is a skilled craftsman in home remodel and an outdoor sportsman. His life companion, Chris Anderson is an experienced direct-response marketing manager. He and Chris are well traveled by motorcycle. Steve left hockey many years ago and found golf. Steve's daughter Rebecca has earned a Degree in Vocal Performance from BYU and is planning a master's program in non-profit business management at U. Illinois-Chicago. Daughter Katherine is in specialty retailing with a firm in the state of Idaho.

Son Dave attended the U of Minnesota and joined United Parcel Service at age 18. He is an accomplished outdoor hunting/fishing sportsman, an excellent mechanic and home maintenance technician. He has shared in the ownership and management of rental properties with Sandy and I for over 30 years. Dave's wife Betty Scott O'Neil has a background in retail, retail banking and as a teacher aid. Their son Nick is an accomplished golfer and daughter Megan is currently completing her undergraduate work at Bethel U in St Paul with a major in Math and a minor in Business.

Daughter Sara is a graduate of Gustavus Adolphus College in St Peter, Minnesota. She is a licensed insurance representative employed by the inside agency of the large Central States Ag Coop, CENEX. Husband Rich Fish is an accomplished home remodeler and motor nut. The family is quite involved in biking. Daughter

Sandy Jean is a 7th grader, excellent student, voracious reader and competitive in Karate and Biking.

Sandy's brother, Mike Tietge, 1962 graduate of the US Air Force Academy, is retired Military with 20 years in the US Air Force as an F-4 Fighter Pilot. He served in Viet Nam. Unfortunately, Mike lost his wife Terry to Cancer a few years ago. He currently lives in Northern Arizona, has two adult children Mark and Jill living in Phoenix.

Sandy's second brother Dennis and his wife MaryJo are retired, split their time between Wausau, Wisconsin, where they lived for many years, and Sun City, Arizona. Dennis was a teacher, golfer and Curling Coach in Wausau, MaryJo is a medical technologist and worked in the Wausau medical circuit for many years. Their children, Rosemary in California, Joel Tietge and his family in the Madison, Wisconsin, area and Betsy Daniels and her family in the Milwaukee area,

Cheryl, Sandy's younger sister completed a Dental Hygiene Degree at the Marquette University, School of Dentistry in Milwaukee. She practiced for twenty years in Minnesota before her marriage to Dr Kenneth Riley of Hiawatha, Kansas. She and Dr Riley live in Hiawatha, spend many months in Arizona and travel extensively throughout the world.

IT'S A WRAP!

The O'Neil's of Cromane, County Kerry, lived in Cheshire County, New Hampshire, and in London, Ontario, Canada, for nearly 30 years after immigrating to North America. In the 1880's they relocated for the final time to follow a pioneer lifestyle in Polk and Burnett Counties in Northwest Wisconsin. There, their son, my Grandpa, Charles Francis O'Neil, b1871 in Canada, discovered Margaret (Maggie) Orr, b1872 in Wisconsin, the daughter of another Pioneer family, the James Orr family. The Orr roots were in England, Scotland and Ireland. The Orrs had arrived in Polk Co. Wisconsin in the 1860's after years of hardship in the state of Maine.

My mother's family the Boliers, were French Canadian who lived in Quebec and the state of Maine before arriving in Pierce Co. Wisconsin and Spring Valley in the 1880's. Grandpa Fred Bolier met Delia Duhamel, a lady with French Canadian roots in Wisconsin, they married, and my mother, Florence, was their second child. Unfortunately, my Grandmother Delia was a victim of early on-set heart disease, and as a young woman my Mother was in charge of managing the family for many years.

My family, including the O'Neil's, Orr's and Bolier's, commonly live into their 80's and 90's. That's good news for later generations. The game changers are accidents and alcohol along the way. Sandy's family, the Tietge's and the Miller's are long livers, as well.

Now in early 2019, Sandy is 82, I am 83. We have been retired for 20 years and living a quiet and comfortable life in Minnesota. We just celebrated our 61st wedding anniversary in December with family and friends. We have no life-threatening diseases and are in good health. I have required replacement of hips and knees and get along quite well with the man-made replacements. Sandy has had occasional bouts with Colitis and a nasty surgery requiring abdominal opening. But all is under control and not limiting our life style. We are able to come and go at will, have no debt, comfortable net worth, a comfortable home, travel wherever and whenever we choose. We have great friends, though fewer each year.

Our family is nearby except for two granddaughters Katie, living in Idaho and Becky in Chicago. The four other grandchildren including Madeline, Nick, Megan O'Neil and Sandy Fish are all in the Twin Cities area. Their parents, Mike and Susanne, Steve and Christine, Dave and Betty, Sara and Rich Fish are all very much a part of the family legacy. And fortunately, all live nearby.

Sandy has stuck with me through thick and thin – from high highs to low lows during our journey together. In our early 50's, we were financially on the edge, but in our mid 60's, we were financially well again and retired on schedule with fully restored resources plus a retirement nest-egg.

I have felt a personal level of self-confidence since I was very young. I was never into recklessness or edgy stuff but confident I could achieve in the American way. Some, who do not understand accepting measured risk, believe entrepreneurial people are risk takers. I disagree; those of us willing to start ventures are accepting risk but generally only in measured amounts. We are not gamblers, we do not buy lottery tickets or bet the horses and visualize how we will spend the winnings. We plan, we organize, we evaluate, we research, we study alternatives, and we have the courage to act with better odds on our side. If we fail, it is not reason to quit trying … but to go forward and not make the same mistakes later. We call it experience. In my life, I have had the opportunity to practice Entrepreneurial, (Outside the corporate umbrella) and Intrapreneurial, (Inside the corporate umbrella) each with their own risks and rewards.

Arthur and Julia O'Neil showed great **courage,** even in the face of the Irish Famine and ruthless British rule to leave their family legacy of hundreds of years in Southwest Ireland and come to North America alone with their little family.

Charlie and Maggie as a team of early pioneers in the valley of the St. Croix River were very **resourceful**. Charlie the stone mason, inventor, award-winning salesman for International Harvester, shopkeeper, stock-yard manager and community lawman, Maggie the school "marm" at an age when she was barely out of school herself.

The **courage** of my Mother and Dad, making tough decisions during the Great Depression, the War years, and the Alcan highway commitment, are all streaming in my life.

The **entrepreneurial** instincts of Fred Bolier, a high achiever in business in both Montana and Western Wisconsin and the same **instincts** found in Billy Orr in building and hacking out his future in tiny Orr, Minnesota, in the early 1900's, furthers my belief that family genes have brought me to this place.

I don't believe all members of the family line inherit the special genes. As I look around through the family, I am certain cousin Marilyn Heebink/Stutt has it. Her autobiography is entitled, "A Different Drummer," and she demonstrates her **courage** and **creativity** multiple times in her book. She comments on luck and divine guidance. I can't argue with that. Cousin Neil Norelius has it. As a young man he took on a business, which would beg for an owner with an engineering background. He had the **courage** and the **instincts** to make the business happen without the professional background necessary, and today, it supports at least six families.

As I had guessed when selecting to minor in psychology in college, business is people as well as product/service. Understanding and predicting human behavior including my own, in transactions of buying, selling, working together, supervising or being supervised is a challenge in the study of human behavior. I admit to being a serial entrepreneur, but also to being a Husband, Dad, Grand-father, Father-in Law, Son, Friend, Cousin, Brother-in-Law, Teacher, Student, Counselor, Advisor and Team-Mate.

It's in the genes, and this is my take on Gene's genes. I did it my way with help of a good wife and family, good genes, good friends, very smart ancestors and … I'm sticking to it!

1345 – O'Neil Castle, County Antrim, Northern Ireland.

1590 – Blennerhasset Castle, now operates as Ballyseedy Castle Hotel near Tralee, County Kerry, Ireland.

A1

1890 – Wisconsin Lumberjacks and their log sled.

1903 – Billy Orr (with vest, standing next to his wife and daughter). Timber baron and founder of the town of Orr, Minnesota, where he owned the general store, the saloon, the hotel and the bank.

1891 – James Orr, Jr., and Margaret Rogers Orr with their daughter, "Maggie," who married Charlie O'Neil and became my grandmother.

1890 – Julia Langford O'Neil, mother of Grandpa Charlie and 12 more.

1907 – Arthur and Julia O'Neil's "tree stump" gravesite, Wolf Creek, Wisconsin.

1945 – Grandpa Charlie and Paddy, the "Wonder Dog."

1950 – Charlie, the Town Constable of St. Croix Falls.

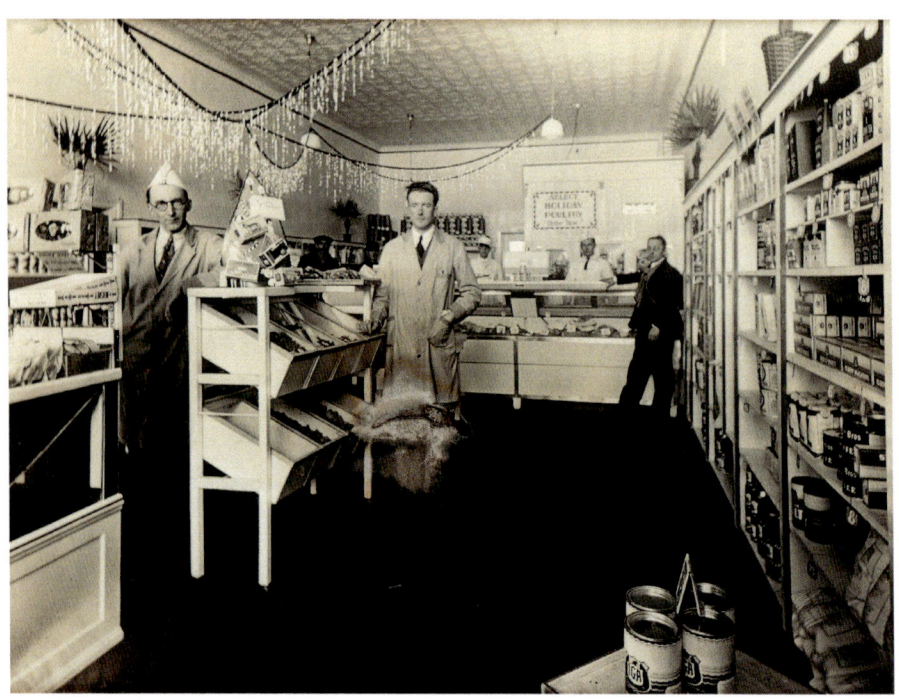

1924 – Charles O'Neil Meat Market, St. Croix Falls, Wisconsin. Gene O'Neil, Senior, in butcher's smock.

1898 – Maggie played the violin, as well as the piano and organ.

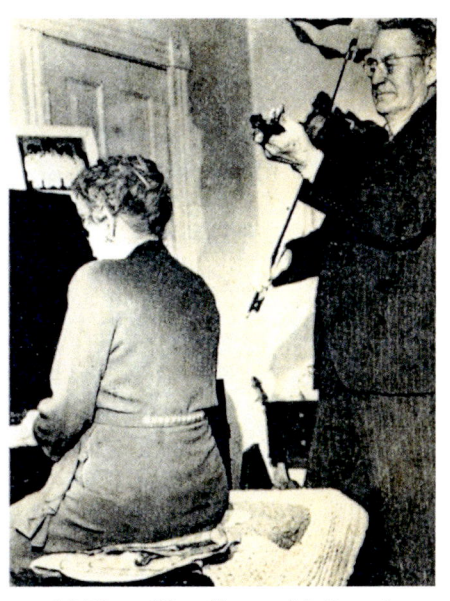

1953 – Charlie and Maggie entertain with some of their "old-time music."

1943 – Charlie and Maggie and their family – daughter Carol and son Gene on the left, and daughter Margaret on the right.

1898 – Fred Bolier, a gentleman on his way up.

1913 – Fred Bolier & family, Ballentine, Montana. Merchant, hotel keeper, livery and stage line to Billings. Front row children L-R: Florence, Marge, Hazel, Evie and Lloyd. Back row, L-R: Fred, Unk., Unk., Delia.

1943 – Visiting my Heebink cousins, Marilyn, Nancy, Georgia and Gail on their farm in Baldwin, Wisconsin.

1941 – Gene (6) and Billy Bonesho (7), friends for life in Eau Claire, Wisconsin.

1954 – Airman, and US Air Force "Globemaster."

1957 – Sandy: new Registered nurse.

A8

1953 – Graduate of Eau Claire Sr. High.

1954 – Sandy: High School Honor Graduate and soon a student nurse.

1947 – Maggie and Charlie on their 50th wedding anniversary. All here except Mike Heebink, who had to leave early.

A9

1957 – Gene (22) and Sandy (21) on their
Wedding Day, December 28.

1957 – O'Neil and Tietge families united.

1961 – BS in Business Ad, U of Wisconsin, Eau Claire.

1957 – Four generations of O'Neils. Great Grandma Maggie (87), Grandpa Gene (54), Dad Gene (24) and baby Mike (3 months).

1964 – Delighted that a brother for Mike and Steve is on the way.

A11

1977 – Smooching on the sofa on our 20th wedding anniversary.

1975 – October 6, Dad's birthday and his final trip to the Jack Pines hunting cabin.

1973 – All the growing family, including "Pepper."

1980 – Energy Shed IPO: Jerry Alstead, Underwriter, Ted B., Partner.

1982 – The Energy Shed: Minnesota Business Journal centerfold.

A13

FRANCHISE FORUM

Franchise Consulting • Training • Management

F.E. Gene O'Neil
President - Senior Consultant
612-481-0101

The Consultant.    1985 – Launched consulting venture, "Franchise Forum, Inc."

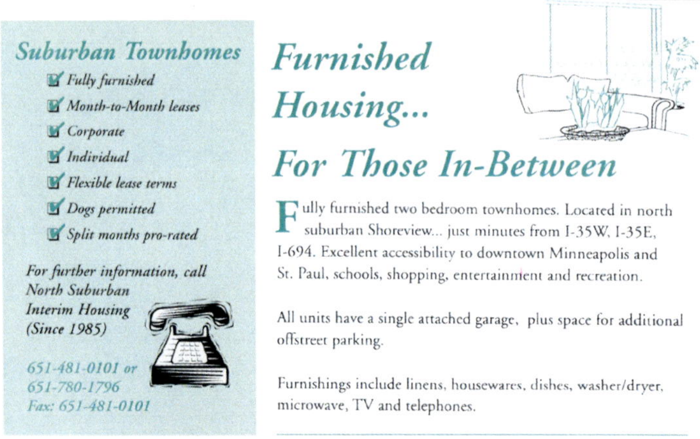

Suburban Townhomes
- Fully furnished
- Month-to-Month leases
- Corporate
- Individual
- Flexible lease terms
- Dogs permitted
- Split months pro-rated

For further information, call
North Suburban
Interim Housing
(Since 1985)

651-481-0101 or
651-780-1796
Fax: 651-481-0101

Furnished Housing...
For Those In-Between

Fully furnished two bedroom townhomes. Located in north suburban Shoreview... just minutes from I-35W, I-35E, I-694. Excellent accessibility to downtown Minneapolis and St. Paul, schools, shopping, entertainment and recreation.

All units have a single attached garage, plus space for additional offstreet parking.

Furnishings include linens, housewares, dishes, washer/dryer, microwave, TV and telephones.

1986 – Launched a new real estate venture, "North Suburban Interim Housing," offering fully furnished, two-bedroom townhomes with short terms.

1990 – The "trendy" family.

2000 – "Like" sisters, Gail Skinner, Georgia Clausen, Nancy Mason, Marilyn Stutt. (All Heebink cousins.)

2000 – "Like" brothers, Bill Bonesho, George Losby, Tom Hanson, and Bob Neperud.

2000 – "Like" brother, Jack Allison, (in the back).

2002 – Another of my "like" brothers – Jim Scolman with Marilyn.

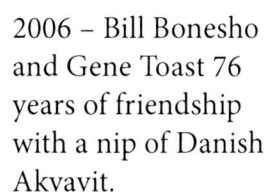

2006 – Bill Bonesho and Gene Toast 76 years of friendship with a nip of Danish Akvavit.

2007 – Cousins Jay and Neil Norelius, Georgia Clausen, and Gene celebrate common family roots.

2012 – Five Irishmen at the Jack Pine hunting lodge: Mike, Dave, Steve, Nick and Gene.

1986 – Five bucks on opening day at the Jack Pines Hunting lodge. Hunters O'Neils, Allisons, Bergstrom, Pater, Dennis Tietge, and Tracy Nelson.

2002 – Retired and loving it!

2004 – Duggan, a great friend, lived over 16 years.

2002 – We enjoy spending part of our retirement time at our Red Cedar Lake House in Birchwood, Wisconsin.

2000 – "Grumpy Old Men," Jack Allison and Gene

2008 – My personal best: 28-3/4 inch, 9+ pound Walleye from NW Ontario.

2012 – All in the Family.

A21

2015 – Visiting the Normandy Beaches of France.

2015 – St. Colomb's Cathedral. An old (1633) Church of Ireland (COI), located inside the walled city of Derry, (Londonderry), Northern Ireland.

2015 – At a Dublin Pub for an Irish dinner/show: Maddie, Susanne, Sandy's cousin, Carol Lundstrom, Sandy, Mike and Gene.

2017 – Friends Kenny and Heather Moore, Coleraine, Northern Ireland.

2017 – Our 60th anniversary. What a fast trip this has been!

FAMILY TREES

O'NEIL FAMILY TREE

Edward Neill, son of Alexander Neill (1763-1827), was born in 1797 in Cromane, Killorglin, Co. Kerry, Ireland, and died there in 1877. In February 1804, in the Kerry Parish Church, Parochial Area of Kilcolman, he married **Lucy Blennerhasset.** The daughter of Sir Rowland Blennerhasset, Lucy was born in 1783 in Blennerville, Co. Kerry, and died on an unknown date. They had four children.

The Children of Edward Neill and Lucy Blennerhasset:

Bridget Neill, born 2 October 1805 in Cromane, County Kerry. She married William Daly.

James O'Neill, Born 16 December 1807 in Cromane, County Kerry.

Robert O'Neill was born 8 September 1810 in County Kerry, Ireland and died on an unknown date.

Arthur A. Charles O'Neil, an Episcopalian, was born on 11 March 1819 in County Kerry, Ireland. He married **Julia Langford,** a Catholic. Twice. **Julia,** daughter of John Francis Langford and Ellen O'Conner, was born on 16 December 1827 in Killarney, Ireland. **Arthur** and **Julia** were married in the Roman Catholic Church at Castlemaine, Co. Kerry on 22 January 1846. A second marriage took place in The Church of Ireland, Kiltallagh Parish, on 31 January 1846. They came to America in 1847. **Arthur** died on 9 May 1905, and **Julia** died on 9 October 1907. They are buried at Wolf Creek Cemetery, Sterling, Wisconsin. They had thirteen children.

The Children of Arthur O'Neil and Julia Langford:

William F. O'Neil was born in 1845 in Killarney, Ireland, and died on an unknown date. He Married **Mary Reason**. They had six children.

The Children of William O'Neil and Mary Reason:

Julia O'Neil
Margaret O'Neil
Caroline O'Neil
John O'Neil
Pauline O'Neil
William Joseph O'Neil

Edward A. O'Neil was born in 1846 in Killarney, Ireland, and died on an unknown date. He married **Bridget,** who was born in 1848 and died on an unknown date. They had five children.

The Children of Edward O'Neil and Bridget:

Julia O'Neil
Willie O'Neil
Nellie O'Neil
Edward O'Neil
Hanna O'Neil

Stanford O'Neil was born in London, Ontario, Canada, and died on an unknown date.

Lucy Ellen O'Neil was born about 1851 in London, Ontario, Canada, and died on 4 May 1886.

James H. O'Neil was born on 2 April 1853 in Keene, Cheshire, New Hampshire, and died on 9 September 1929 in Minneapolis, Minnesota. He married **Eva Fowler**. The had three children.

The Children of James O'Neil and Eva Fowler:

Arthur O'Neil
John O'Neil
Henry James O'Neil

Arthur A. O'Neil was born on 7 April 1861 in Keene, NH, and died on 3 March 1932 in Crow Wing County,

Minnesota. He married **Mrs. Sarah Smith Wilson** in 1884. They moved to Aitkin, Minnesota in 1891. **Sarah** died in 1929. They had five children.

The Children of Arthur O'Neil and Sarah Smith:

Roy O'Neil
Percy O'Neil
Guy O'Neil
James O'Neil
Gertrude O'Neil

Ann O'Neil was born on 10 May 1866 in London, Ontario, Canada, and died on an unknown date. She lived in Everett, Washington in 1932.

Elizabeth Louise O'Neil was born in 20 February 1867 in Keene, Cheshire, New Hampshire, and died on 23 November 1935 in London, Ontario, Canada. She married **Henry Allen Holden** on 7 June 1900 in Woodstock, Ontario, Canada. **Henry Allen** was born in 1876 and died in 1939 in London, Ontario, Canada.

Alexander G. O'Neil was born on 28 February 1868 in Keene, Cheshire, New Hampshire, and died on an unknown date. He lived in St. Paul, Minnesota in 1932.

Alice O'Neil was born in 1869 in Keene, New Hampshire, and died on an unknown date. She lived in Osceola, Wisconsin, in 1932.

Charles Francis O'Neil was born on 27 March 1871 in London, Ontario, Canada, and died on 7 July 1954 in St. Croix Falls, Wisconsin. He married **Margaret L. (Maggie) Orr** on 4 May 1897 in Sterling Wisconsin. **Margaret,** daughter of James Orr, Jr. and Margaret Rogers, was born on 15 September 1872 in Sterling, Wisconsin, and died on 6 May 1963 in St. Croix Falls, Wisconsin. They had three children.

The Children of Charles O'Neil and Margaret Orr

Margaret Julia O'Neil was born on 5 June 1908 in St. Croix Falls, Wisconsin, and died on 30 January 2000 in Albuquerque, New Mexico. She married **Myron Lawrence Heebink,** who was born on 25 September 1903 in Baldwin, Wisconsin, and died on 26 June 1982 in Albuquerque, New Mexico. They had four children.

Children of Margaret O'Neil and Myron Heebink:

Marilyn Jean Heebink was born on Aug. 25, 1927 in St. Croix Falls, Wisconsin.

Nancy Carol Heebink was born on May 1, 1930 in Baldwin, Wisconsin, and died May 25, 2016, in Oceanside, California.

Georgia Margaret Heebink was born on Mar. 8, 1932 in Baldwin, Wisconsin.

Gail Patricia Heebink was born on Nov. 5, 1939 in Baldwin, Wisconsin.

Carol Rebecca O'Neil was born on 25 December 1910 in St. Croix Falls, Wisconsin, and died on 12 April 2006 in Lindstrom, Minnesota. **Carol** married **Paul Sigfrid Norelius** on Aug. 8, 1937. The son of Marion Sigfrid Norelius and Alice Youngberg, **Paul** was born on 29 April 1910 and died on 16 October 1990 in Lindstrom, Minnesota.

Children of Carol O'Neil and Paul Norelius:

Neil Sigfrid Norelius was born on 5 September 1938 in Lindstrom, Minnesota.

Jay Paul Norelius was born on 9 March 1941 in Lindstrom, Minnesota.

Francis Eugene O'Neil, Sr. was born on 6 October 1905 in St. Croix Falls, Wisconsin and died 17 November 1975, in Eau Claire, Wisconsin. He married Florence Marie Bolier on 14 July 1933. The daughter of Fred Bolier and Dahlia Duhamel, **Florence** was born 3 April 1908 in Baldwin, Wisconsin, and died on 17 November 1975 in Baldwin, Wisconsin. They had one child.

Children of Francis Eugene O'Neil and Florence Bolier:

Francis Eugene O'Neil, Jr. was born on 2 March 1935 in St. Croix Falls, Wisconsin. He married **Sandra Lou Tietge** on 28 December 1957 in Eau Claire, Wisconsin. The daughter of Harold Leslie Tietge and Cozette Miller Tietge, **Sandra** was born 21 September 1936 in Sioux Falls, South Dakota. They had four children.

Children of Francis E. O'Neil, Jr., and Sandra Tietge:

Michael Eugene O'Neil was born 27 May 1959 in Eau Claire, Wisconsin. He married **Susanne Busse** on 5 October 1992. **Susanne** was born November 17, 1952 in Minneapolis, Minnesota.

Steven Leslie O'Neil was born 9 August 1961 in Eau Claire, Wisconsin. He married **Sheila Reynolds** on 27 December 1987. They were divorced and he then married **Kellene Voegele** on 5 July 1997. They were divorced in May 2004.

David Charles O'Neil was born 12 May 1964 in St. Paul, Minnesota. He married **Betty Jane Scott** on April 3, 1993. **Betty Jane** was born 23 May 1964 in St. Paul, Minnesota.

Sara Beth O'Neil was born 14 February 1970 in St. Paul, Minnesota. She was adopted by **Francis Eugene** and **Sandra O'Neil** on 18 March 1970. **Sara** married **Richard Charles Fish, Jr**. on 30 May 1997. **Richard Fish, Jr**. was born 12 October 1970 in St. Paul, Minnesota.

ORR FAMILY TREE

James Orr, Sr., was born in 1798 near Manchester, England. He married **Margaret Carmichael** of Dundee, Scotland, and, in 1820, they immigrated to Aroostook County, Maine. Margaret soon died and, in 1822, he married her sister, **Jane Carmichael,** who was born in 1799 in Dundee, Scotland. They are buried in Aroostook County, Maine.

The Children of James Orr, Sr. and Jane Carmichael

James Orr, Jr., was born 24 June 1828 in Aroostook County, Maine, near Haynesville. He married **Margaret Rogers** on 24 June 1851 in a Baptist church in Aroostook County, Maine. Margaret was born 30 April 1828 in Manchester, England. In 1864, they moved to a homestead in Sterling, Wisconsin. Margaret died 12 January 1904, and James died 31 March 1915. They are buried in the Wolf Creek Cemetery, Sterling, Wisconsin. They had 13 children.

The Children of James Orr, Jr., and Margaret Rogers:

Sarah Orr was born in Aroostook County, Maine, on 9 February 1853. She married **George Emery**. Sarah died on 22 January 1904 and is buried in the Wolf Creek Cemetery, Sterling, Wisconsin.

The Children of Sarah Orr and George Emery:

George Emery, Jr.
Rose Emery
Adah Emery
Cyrus Emery
Jessie Emery

Jane Orr was born in Aroostook County, Maine, on 7 April 1854. She married **Ben Gore**, a French Canadian, who died on an unknown date. They had two children. After Gore's death, **Jane** married

Henry Worth. They had four children. **Jane** died 9 June 1904 and is buried in the Wolf Creek Cemetery, Sterling, Wisconsin.

The Children of Jane Orr and Ben Gore:

Ella Gore
Sadie Gore

The Children of Jane Orr and Henry Worth:

Lulu Worth
Edna Worth
Paul Worth
Myra Worth

Eliza Orr was born in Aroostook County, Maine, on 1 December 1855. She married **Henry Emery.** They had eight children. She died 21 September 1950 in Eveleth, Wisconsin, and is buried there.

The Children of Eliza Orr and Henry Emery:

William Emery
Harry Emery
Samuel Emery
Charles Emery
John Emery
Thomas Emery
Cyrus Emery
Maggie Emery

Mary Orr was born 16 March in Aroostook County, Maine. She married **William Doty**. They had six children. She died 8 November 1938 in Medford, Oregon, and is buried there.

William (Billy) Orr was born in Aroostook County, Maine, on 19 May 1857. His twin brother, John, died at birth. He married **Ella Harvey.** They had two children. They divorced in the 1980's. In 1897, he married **Josephine Lumbar.** They adopted a daughter. Billy and Josephine both died in 1933 and are buried in the Calvary Cemetery, Virginia, Minnesota.

The Children of William Orr and Ella Harvey:

Ruby Orr
George Orr

The Children of William Orr and Josephine Lumbar:

Patricia Orr

Rebecca Orr was born in Aroostook County, Maine, on 17 April 1861. She married **George Churchill.** Rebecca died 15 July 1938 in Osceola, Wisconsin, and is buried in the St. Croix Falls Cemetery. They had five children.

The Children of Rebecca Orr and George Churchill:

Charlie and **Bertha Churchill**
George Churchill, Jr.
Pearl Churchill
Neil Churchill

Rachel Orr was born 27 March 1863 in Aroostook County, Maine. She married **William Perkins** of Hastings, Minnesota. She died on 18 May 1940. They had two children.

The Children of Rachel Orr and William Perkins:

Russell Perkins
Roy Perkins

Grace Evaline Orr was born 16 May 1864 in Aroostook County, Maine. On 25 October 1882, she married **Richard Henry Barter**, who was born 23 October 1851 in Quebec, Canada. Grace died 22 May 1933 in Milwaukee, Wisconsin. They had ten children.

The Children of Grace Orr and Richard Barter:

David Elsworth Barter
Francis Dean Barter
Eva Myrtle Barter
James Orr Barter
Arthur Marion Barter
Benjamin Thomas Barter
Leon Russell Barter
Morrell Leroy Barter
Margaret Genevieve Barter
Dorothy Rebecca Barter

Thomas Rogers Orr was born 22 April 1867 in Sterling Township, Wisconsin. He married **Mae Cragen** 17 May 1870. He died on 4 November 1943. Mae died on 27 May 1946. They are buried in the Wolf Creek Cemetery near St. Croix Falls, Wisconsin. They had five children.

The Children of Thomas Orr and Mae Cragen:

Hugh Cragen
Russell Cragen
Howard Cragen
Lucy Cragen
Myrtle Cragen

James Douglas Orr was born 19 February 1869 at Meadows Homestead in Sterling, Wisconsin. He married **Lucy** in 1898. They had no children. He died on 22 December 1956. He and Lucy are buried in a mausoleum in Spokane, Washington. They had no children.

Margaret L. (Maggie) Orr was born 15 September 1872 at Meadow Homestead in Sterling Township, Wisconsin. On 4 May 1897, she married **Charles Francis O'Neil**, who was born on 27 March 1871 in London, Ontario, Canada. **Charles** died 7 July 1954, and **Maggie** passed away 6 May 1963. **Maggie** and **Charles** are buried in the St. Croix Falls, Wisconsin Cemetery. They had three children.

The Children of Maggie Orr and Charles O'Neil:

Francis Eugene O'Neil, Sr. was born on 6 October 1905 in St. Croix Falls, Wisconsin, and died 17 November 1975, in Eau Claire, Wisconsin. He married **Florence Marie Bolier**, who was born 3 April 1908 and died on 17 November 1975 in Baldwin, Wisconsin.

Margaret Julia O'Neil was born on 5 June 1908 in St. Croix Falls, Wisconsin, and died on 30 January 2000 in Albuquerque, New Mexico. She married **Myron Lawrence Heebink**, who was born on 25 September 1903 in Baldwin, Wisconsin, and died on 26 June 1982 in Albuquerque, New Mexico.

Carol Rebecca O'Neil was born on 25 December 1910 in St. Croix Falls, Wisconsin, and died on 12 April 2006 in Lindstrom, Minnesota. She married **Paul Sigfrid Norelius,** who was born on 29 April 1910 and died on 16 October 1990 in Lindstrom, Minnesota.

Sammie Orr was born 11 May 1874 and passed away 13 December 1882 with diphtheria.

BOLIER FAMILY TREE

The **Beaulieu** family, originally from France, immigrated to Quebec, Canada, in the early 1800's. There, they changed their name from Beaulieu to Bolier.

Peter (Pierre) Bolier, son of Edwin and Julia Bolier (Beaulieu), was born in 1830 in Quebec, Canada. In 1840, when Peter was 16 years old, the family relocated to Old Town, Penobscot, Maine. Here, on 30 October 1864, Peter married **Ellen Delina Willett** (1840-1923). Around 1885, they relocated to Minneapolis, Minnesota, and then to Gilman, Pierce County, Wisconsin. Peter was killed in an industrial accident on 1 July 1905. He was buried in a small cemetery near Spring Valley, Wisconsin.

Children of Peter Bolier and Delina Willett:

Peter Bolier, born in 1870
Mary Bolier, born in 1872
Ellen Bolier, born in 1875

Freddie (Fred) Bolier, was born 10 December 1878 in Old Town, Maine, and died 19 August 1960 in Baldwin, Wisconsin. In 1903, he married **Delia Duhamel,** daughter of Finley and Zoe Duhamel, who was born in 1881 and died in 1930.

Children of Fred Bolier and Delia Duhamel:

Lloyd Francis Bolier, born 26 October 1907 in Baldwin, Wisconsin, and died 18 October 1947. He married **Esther Genevieve Gunvalson**.

Hazel Bolier, born 25 August 1909 in Baldwin, Wisconsin, and died 7 November 1995. She married **Vic Mallongree.**

Evelyn Bolier, born 6 May 1912 in Baldwin, Wisconsin, and died 30 April 1993. She married **Bernard (Red) Norwick.**

Margorie Katherine Bolier, born 3 April 1915 in Ballentine, Montana, and died 21 December 2997. She married **William Gavin**.

Edith Lucille Bolier, born 28 August 1917 in Baldwin, Wisconsin, and died 9 February 2007. She married **Roy Nelson.**

Donald L. Bolier born 26 January 1923 in Baldwin, Wisconsin, and died 20 January 1962. He married **Dorothy Nieterer**.

<u>Florence Marie Bolier</u>, was born 3 April 1908 in Baldwin, Wisconsin and died 28 July 2002 in Baldwin, Wisconsin. On 14 July 1933, she married **Francis Eugene (Gene) O'Neil**, son of Charles and Maggie O'Neil of St. Croix Falls, Wisconsin, who was born 6 October 1905 in St. Croix Falls, Wisconsin, and died 17 November 1975 in Eau Claire, Wisconsin. They had one child.

> **Children of Florence Bolier and Francis Eugene O'Neil Sr.:**
>
> <u>**Francis Eugene (Gene) O'Neil, Jr.**</u> was born on 2 March 1935 in St. Croix Falls, Wisconsin. On 28 December 1957, he married **Sandra Lou Tietge** in Eau Claire, Wisconsin. Sandra, the daughter of Harold Tietge and Cozette Miller Tietge, was born 21 September 1936 in Sioux Falls, South Dakota. They had four children.
>
>> **Children of Francis Eugene O'Neil, Jr., and Sandra Tietge:**
>>
>> **Michael Eugene O'Neil** was born 27 May 1959 in Eau Claire, Wisconsin.
>>
>> **Steven Leslie O'Neil** was born 9 August 1961 in Eau Claire, Wisconsin.

David Charles O'Neil was born 12 May 1964 at in St. Paul, Minnesota.

Sara Beth O'Neil was born 14 February 1970 in St. Paul, Minnesota. She was adopted on 18 March 1970.